JOHN MCHOOK

# Become
# VISTAREADY

## HOW TO PREPARE FOR THE SEASON OF ADVENTURES

2025 EDITION

# Become VistaReady: How to prepare for the season of adventures. 2025 Edition.

Copyright © 2025
John McHook
VistaReady LLC

# Table of Contents

Introduction: Welcome to VistaReady   4

**Part I: Building the Right Mindset**   9

Chapter 1: The Call of Adventure   10

Chapter 2: Identifying & Tackling Mental Barriers   15

Chapter 3: Setting Meaningful Adventure Goals   20

**Part II: The Foundations—Essential Outdoor Basics**   26

Chapter 4: Core Outdoor Skills & Safety   27

Chapter 5: Fundamental Gear & Packing   33

Chapter 5.1: Gear Examples   39

Chapter 6: Planning Logistics & Permits   46

**Part III: Gear, Tech & Monetization**   52

Chapter 7: The Gear Revolution of 2025   53

Chapter 8: Filming & Content Creation   59

Chapter 9: Monetizing Your Outdoor Passion   66

**Part IV: Physical & Mental Conditioning**   73

Chapter 10: Fitness for Adventure   74

Chapter 11: Nutrition & Peak Performance   80

Chapter 11.1: Examples and Recipes for Nutrition & Performance   86

**Part V: Adversity & Advanced Preparedness**   91

Chapter 12: Facing Worst-Case Scenarios   93

Chapter 13: Responsible Adventuring & Community   100

**Part VI: Bringing It All Together**   107

Chapter 14: Crafting Your 2025 Action Plan   110

Chapter 15: Conclusion: Your VistaReady Future   114

# Introduction: Welcome to VistaReady

Close your eyes for a moment and imagine this scene—you're standing atop a rugged hill, the world stretching out before you in every direction. The sunlight warms your skin, the scent of pine fills the air, and the gentle whisper of the wind carries away the noise of everyday life. For a brief moment, everything feels possible. You're fully present, yet somehow, part of something much bigger. That sense of wonder? That urge to explore? That's the power of adventure, and it's waiting for you.

Welcome to **VistaReady**, your guide to unlocking the season of exploration in 2025. This book isn't about climbing the highest peak (though we'll cheer if you do!). It's about tapping into something primal—the shared human need to seek new vistas, both literal and metaphorical. Whether you're a complete newbie to the outdoors, a gear enthusiast, or someone stuck in self-doubt about where to begin, this book is here to help. Your next great adventure isn't only possible—it's closer than you think.

## Why 2025 is Your Year to Begin

Why *now*? The year 2025 is shaping up to be the ultimate adventure playground. The world, as we know it, is shifting. After years of people being stuck in routines, tethered to screens, or feeling weighed down by endless pressures, there's now a collective urge to live more authentically. And for many of us, that means reconnecting with the great outdoors.

Technological advances have made it safer than ever to step into the wild. Lightweight gear, smart tech, and eco-friendly designs mean you can be better prepared and more connected without being bogged down. At the same time, there's a growing movement toward balance—people want meaningful experiences over material things. Time spent outdoors isn't just a pastime anymore; it's an investment in your health, your clarity, and your overall happiness.

Whether you're itching to explore a local trail or dreaming of globe-trotting expeditions, there's never been a better moment to lace up your boots, grab your pack, and say yes to adventure. And here's the kicker—you don't have to do it all perfectly. Starting small is still starting, and every single step counts.

## What Does "VistaReady" Mean?

At its heart, being **VistaReady** is about so much more than outdoor skills or packing the right gear. It's a mindset—a way of approaching life with three core principles:

1. **Optimism** – The outdoors teaches us that challenges are stepping stones, not stumbling blocks. Optimism isn't blind faith; it's the belief that you can grow with each obstacle you encounter. An unexpected thunderstorm might drench your hike, but it also delivers an unforgettable story and, maybe, the most stunning double rainbow you've ever seen.
2. **Adaptability** – Fancy plans are great until Mother Nature decides otherwise. A rain-soaked trail? A last-minute campsite change? Life, much like the wilderness, demands flexibility.

When you're adaptable, setbacks turn into opportunities, and you learn to find joy even in Plan B (or Plan C).

3. **Preparedness** – This is the grounding force that makes optimism and adaptability possible. It's about building your toolkit—mentally, physically, and literally—so you can handle the unexpected while still enjoying the ride. Preparedness isn't just about avoiding bad outcomes; it's about anticipating the best.

**VistaReady** isn't a finish line; it's a way of living. It's about seeing the world differently—whether you're gazing out over a mountain range or making fresh discoveries in your own backyard.

## What This Book Will Teach You

If the idea of hiking through untouched forests or camping under starlit skies feels thrilling but *also* intimidating, you're not alone. Many of us weren't raised in outdoor-focused environments, and it's easy to think, "That's not for me. I wasn't born adventurous." But here's the truth—it's for everyone. You don't need to climb Everest to call yourself an adventurer. Your first five-mile trail is just as valid as a three-week trek in the Andes.

This book will guide you, step by step, through everything you need to know to thrive outdoors. We'll cover the practical, the personal, and even a bit of the philosophical.

Here's what each part dives into:

- **The Mindset:** Many adventures begin in your head. We'll explore how curiosity can overpower doubt, how to set goals that truly matter, and how to cultivate your confidence for every step of the way.
- **The Basics:** From navigation and essential gear to trip logistics, you'll learn how to make the outdoors feel less overwhelming and much more approachable. Plus, practical

tips for traveling solo or with a group, no matter your comfort level.

- **The Gear Revolution:** The gear of 2025 isn't like your parents' old camping gear—it's smarter, lighter, and more sustainable. We'll explore which devices, tools, and materials can enhance your experience without weighing you down.
- **Training & Conditioning:** Adventure requires a strong body and mind. That doesn't mean you have to run marathons or adopt extreme workout regimens—we'll cover simple, practical ways to prepare your body and fuel it with the right nutrients.
- **Facing the Tough Stuff:** Not every moment outdoors is Instagram-perfect. We'll explore strategies for handling challenges like navigating bad weather, facing emergency scenarios, and staying resilient when things get tough.
- **Your 2025 Action Plan:** The last chapter will tie it all together, helping you map out your personal adventure goals, find resources, and sustain your momentum beyond a single season.

## Why You Were Made for Adventure

Here's an important reminder as you begin this book: Adventure is not about proving anything to anyone. It's about discovery—of the world, the landscapes, and most importantly, yourself. It's about finding joy in fresh air, new challenges, and the satisfaction of tackling something you once thought was impossible.

You don't need to be an outdoors expert to get started. You're not required to summit mountains or film viral travel vlogs (unless you want to, of course!). Adventure isn't a competition. It's a slow, steady practice of leaning into the unknown, letting nature teach you new things, and learning to trust your own instincts.

If you've been waiting for the perfect day to start exploring—this is it. Turn the next page, take a deep breath, and take that first step. Welcome to the adventure you've been waiting for.

**Key Takeaways**

1. **The Time is Now** – With 2025 offering cutting-edge tools, shifting priorities, and renewed outdoor interest, this is your perfect moment to start exploring.
2. **VistaReady is a Lifestyle** – It's about optimism, adaptability, and preparation—skills that serve you in the wild and beyond.
3. **You Can Start Small** – Adventure doesn't have to be extreme. Even a simple walk in nature can ignite your explorer's spirit.
4. **This is Your Roadmap** – Whether it's mindset, skills, gear, or confidence-building, this book will guide you toward lasting adventures.

Now, the question isn't **if** you're ready to get started, but **how.** Remember, every breathtaking view starts with a single step. And you? You're about to take it.

# Part I: Building the Right Mindset

# Chapter 1: The Call of Adventure

You've heard it before—"The mountains are calling, and I must go." But what is it about those words that gives us a little nudge in the chest, like they're speaking directly to us? Why does the thought of stepping into the unknown stir something inside, even if it feels like a distant, impossible dream?

Adventure is part of us. It's baked into our DNA. From the first humans who wandered over mountains and across seas, to the astronauts staring into the vast unknown of space, the desire to explore is as old as time itself. It's not just about seeing new places. It's about becoming someone new in the process.

## Why We Crave New Challenges and Vistas

Maybe you've felt it before—a moment of pause when you're staring out a car window, gazing at a mountain range. Or when you scroll through a photo of someone kayaking on a crystal-blue lake, and you think, *I wish I could do that.* That's your call of adventure. It's subtle, but it's real.

On the surface, it might seem like a craving for a pretty view or a bit of excitement, but on a deeper level, it's about connection. The outdoors connects you to something much bigger than yourself. It turns down the noise of the modern world and gives your brain the freedom to settle, to breathe. Climbing a trail or navigating unfamiliar terrain gives you a sense of accomplishment you can't duplicate on a screen. It reminds you of your own strength, your resilience, your capacity to grow.

And the best part? Nature doesn't require you to be perfect. The trail doesn't ask if you're fit enough, young enough, or fearless enough. It just asks that you take the first step.

## The Voices of Doubt

But here's the thing about the call of adventure—it doesn't always shout. Sometimes, it's just a whisper, and it's easy to drown out with excuses and self-doubt.

- **"I'm not outdoorsy enough."**
  News flash: Nobody is born knowing how to pitch a tent or read a map. Every "outdoorsy" person you've seen was once a beginner. It's not about living in a mountain cabin or owning the fanciest gear. It's about curiosity—and that's something you already have.
- **"I don't have the time."**
  The truth is, life will always pull you in a dozen directions. But making time for adventure doesn't mean taking off for weeks on end. A two-hour Saturday hike can be just as fulfilling as a cross-country expedition. Start small, and you'll quickly realize how those little moments add up.
- **"What if I'm not good at it?"**
  Good at what, exactly? There's no such thing as being "good" at reconnecting with nature. Maybe you get lost following a trail map, or maybe it rains on your first camping trip, but the

beauty lies in the imperfection. You'll laugh about these moments later—and they'll make the victories even sweeter.

## Your Inner Explorer is Waiting

Think back to when you were a kid. Did you climb trees and imagine you were exploring a jungle, or tiptoe along a stream pretending you were discovering uncharted lands? That spirit of wonder—that sense of play—is still inside you. The problem is, as adults, we tell ourselves we need to grow out of it.

But here's the truth: Rekindling that childlike curiosity is a skill, and like any skill, it gets easier with practice. The good news? You don't need to quit your job, find a sherpa, or even leave your zip code to get started.

## Small Shifts to Spark Big Motivation

Getting outdoors and answering your call to adventure doesn't require a total life overhaul. Sometimes it's about building momentum with small shifts that change how you think and feel. Here's how to start:

1. **Reframe Fear as Excitement:**
    Nervousness and excitement are two sides of the same coin. Next time you think, "What if I mess up?" try flipping it to, "What if I discover something amazing?" The jitters mean you're doing something that matters.
2. **Start Close to Home:**
    If full-blown wilderness experiences feel a million miles away, start nearby. Visit your local park, try a short day trip to a nature reserve, or explore a beginner-friendly trail you've never heard of. Adventure doesn't have to mean far away—it just has to mean *new*.
3. **Commit to a Curious Mindset:**
    Instead of asking, "Can I do this?" try asking, "What can I

learn from this?" Curiosity is a powerful antidote to doubt. Shift your focus from fear of failing to an eagerness to experience the unknown.

4. **Find Quick Wins:**

   Short, manageable goals build momentum. Plan a 30-minute nature walk after work. Research one potential weekend hike. These small victories stack up and spark your enthusiasm for bigger adventures.

## Real-Life Inspiration

When Maya first heard her call to adventure, she almost ignored it. She was a self-proclaimed "city girl," someone who didn't own hiking boots and had never used a map. But one day, feeling burnt out, she decided to visit a nearby trail. "It felt silly," she admitted, "because I didn't know what I was doing. But that 3-mile loop changed everything." Unable to resist the satisfaction she felt afterward, Maya began exploring more trails, eventually leading a group hike in Yellowstone two years later.

Her story isn't unique—every adventure lover started with that first hesitant step. Yours could be next.

## Recap – Key Points

1. Adventure is woven into human history. The urge to explore isn't just natural—it's transformational.
2. Self-doubt is normal, but it doesn't have to define you. The trail doesn't care if you're "outdoorsy"; it welcomes everyone.
3. Small choices can make a huge difference. Starting nearby, adopting curiosity, and celebrating small wins are all ways to answer your call to adventure.

## Action Steps

1. Write down one outdoor experience you've always wanted to try—big or small.
2. Plan a tiny "test adventure" for this week, like a walk in the nearest park or a visit to a new trail.
3. Practice reframing doubts into things you're excited to learn or discover. "What if I don't know how to do it?" becomes "I can't wait to see how I figure it out."
4. Find a photo, video, or story of an outdoor adventure that inspires you. Save it as a reminder of why your own adventure matters.

Answering the call of adventure doesn't happen all at once—it's a collection of tiny decisions that, together, lead to something extraordinary. What decision will you make today? Remember, every big view starts with one first step. It's time to take yours.

# Chapter 2: Identifying & Tackling Mental Barriers

Standing on the edge of adventure can bring two very different feelings. On one hand, there's excitement—images of amazing views, fresh air, and a sense of accomplishment. On the other hand, there's its unwelcome companion—fear. Whether it's fear of heights, encounters with wildlife, failure, or stepping into the unknown, mental barriers often feel like immovable walls blocking the path to adventure. But here's the truth: those walls aren't as solid as they seem. You can break through them with the right tools, perspective, and a willingness to take small steps forward.

**Why We Fear the Unknown**

Our brains are wired to seek safety, which means anything unfamiliar can trigger feelings of fear or discomfort. Stepping into nature—where there are no glowing screens, no flat paved floors, and no chair to lean on—can feel like stepping into chaos. Even seasoned adventurers feel jitters before big trips. The key is to understand fear for what it really is—a signal. It's your mind saying, *This is new. This is uncertain. This matters.*

That signal can be valuable. It keeps you cautious and alert, but it doesn't have to stop you in your tracks. Fear is not a roadblock; it's an invitation to grow.

## Common Mental Barriers

Here are some of the most frequent fears people face, along with how to address them head-on:

- **Fear of Heights**
  For many, the thought of standing at a ledge even a few feet off the ground is paralyzing. The racing heart, the wobbling legs—it's all part of a natural response to perceived danger. Instead of fighting it, acknowledge the fear and work through it incrementally.
  *Try This:* Start small by walking across a safe, elevated structure like a wooden footbridge or observation deck. Focus on your breathing and remind yourself you're in control. Acclimating to height in low-risk scenarios builds confidence over time.
- **Fear of Wildlife**
  Bears, snakes, and all those unseen critters creeping through the trees—wild animals are a top worry for outdoor newbies. But the reality is, most creatures want to avoid you as much as you want to avoid them. Armed with a bit of knowledge and preparation, you can mitigate nearly all risks.
  *Try This:* Learn the local wildlife for areas you plan to visit—both how to avoid them and what to do if you encounter them. For example, carrying bear spray in grizzly country or making noise on trails can significantly reduce concerns.
- **Fear of Failure**
  What if I can't finish the hike? What if I get lost? What if I don't enjoy it? Fear of failure often sneaks in disguised as self-doubt. But here's the secret—failure isn't final. It's how we grow. The key is shifting your mindset to see every setback as

part of the process.
*Try This:* Set tiny goals within the larger goal, like reaching a certain point or completing a section at your own pace. Celebrate each small win as proof you're moving forward, no matter how imperfectly.

- **Fear of the Unknown**

  What will happen out there? What if something goes wrong? This catch-all fear is based on uncertainty, but the antidote is preparation. Knowledge replaces uncertainty with confidence.
  *Try This:* Start with low-risk adventures, like a well-maintained, highly-trafficked trail. Read up on what to bring, wear, and expect so you feel confident when you step outside. The more you familiarize yourself, the less intimidating the unknown becomes.

## Reframing Your Relationship with Fear

Instead of banishing fear, invite it to walk alongside you. Here are techniques to tackle mental barriers using mindfulness and mental fitness:

1. **Self-Talk:**

    You are the narrator of your own story. When negative thoughts creep in—*"You're not good at this" or "This is too much for you"—*replace them with empowering ones like, *"I'm learning something new" or "Every step is progress."*

2. **Visualization:**

    Before stepping into a challenging situation, close your eyes and imagine yourself succeeding. Picture yourself reaching the summit or navigating a tricky trail with ease. This mental rehearsal can make the real experience feel more achievable.

3. **Mini-Challenges:**

    If your fears seem overwhelming, shrink the goal. Instead of a 5-mile hike, try a 1-mile loop first. Instead of camping overnight, pack a picnic for a day trip. Mini-challenges give you quick wins to boost confidence.

4. **Grounding Techniques:**

   When fear takes over, bring yourself back to the present moment. Focus on your breath, take note of your surroundings, and remind yourself that you are safe. A simple mantra, like *"One step at a time,"* can also help maintain calm.

## Real Stories of Overcoming Mental Barriers

- **Emma and Her Fear of Heights**

  Emma always avoided high places. Even climbing a ladder to hang holiday lights made her palms sweat. But after watching friends return from a trip with jaw-dropping photos of a cliffside hike, she felt a deep yearning to experience it herself. She started with short climbs to lookout points at her local park, never pushing herself too far or too fast. A few months later, she joined her friends for the hike she'd once only admired in pictures. "I'll never forget that moment of courage and trust in myself," she says.

- **Malik and the Unknown**

  Malik had always lived in cities, never venturing far from the urban hustle and bustle. Camping felt not only foreign, but terrifying. What if he didn't know how to start a fire? What if he couldn't sleep? What if he got lost? Rather than plan an elaborate trip, he joined a beginner-friendly group camping session at a nearby site. With the help of more experienced campers and plenty of prep, Malik discovered that his fears were manageable—and that the first night under the stars was worth every ounce of effort.

## Recap – Key Points

1. Fear is normal but doesn't have to control you—it's an opportunity for growth.

2. Common barriers like fear of heights, wildlife, or failure can be overcome with preparation, incremental steps, and persistence.
3. Practical tools like self-talk, visualization, and mini-challenges help you reframe fear as a positive force rather than a hindrance.
4. Real-life stories remind us that ordinary people can tackle extraordinary fears when they take small, meaningful steps toward courage.

## Action Steps

1. Write down one fear that's holding you back. Name it and note why it feels intimidating.
2. Create a "mini-challenge" designed to confront your fear in a low-stakes environment (e.g., practice crossing a bridge if you fear heights, visit a park if you fear being outdoors).
3. Practice a self-talk mantra that's designed to calm and empower you, such as *"I am learning"* or *"One step at a time."*
4. Read a story or watch a video about someone overcoming that same fear to remind yourself it's possible.

Fear may be part of the adventure, but it doesn't get to write your story. Every time you challenge a mental barrier—no matter how small—you're taking back the reins. And guess what? With every step forward, fear grows quieter, and your confidence grows louder. Adventure doesn't erase fear; it teaches you that you're bigger than it. Take that first step and watch how far you'll go.

# Chapter 3: Setting Meaningful Adventure Goals

There's something magical about a goal. It turns a vague dream into something tangible, something you can hold in your mind and measure in your actions. Whether you're longing to hike a local trail, summit a mountain, or simply spend more time outside, setting clear and meaningful goals is the bridge between where you are now and where you want to be. But here's the catch—it's not just about making a list of things to tick off. To truly thrive in your season of adventure, your goals need heart. They have to align with what excites you, challenges you, and fills you with purpose.

## Finding Your "Why"

Imagine this. You're standing at the base of a hill. It's not a steep climb, and you have the time and energy to summit. The only question is, *why climb it at all?* The answer dictates everything—how you tackle the challenge, what you take away from it, and whether or not you feel satisfied when you reach the top.

Your "why" is the fuel for your adventure engine. It's what helps you push through the tough stretches and savor the victories. For some, the reason is as simple as joy. They're in it for the thrill of seeing something new, experiencing something fresh, and having stories to tell at the end of the day. Others are after something deeper—connecting to nature or testing their limits, whether physically, mentally, or emotionally.

Take Alex, for instance, a regular office worker who found himself craving movement after years of desk-bound days. His why was fitness. He started with short weekend walks but gradually infused his life with bigger goals—first hiking competitions, then international trekking events. On the other hand, there's Laura, who grew up camping with her grandparents. For her, it's about connection. Being outdoors is a way of remembering her roots and feeling close to what she considers home.

What about you? Are you in this for fun, fitness, emotional clarity, or simply because you want to try? Whatever it is, naming your motivation can bring momentum you didn't even know you needed.

## Short-Term vs. Long-Term Adventures

The road to adventure is rarely a straight sprint. More often, it looks like a winding path with stops along the way. This is where short- and long-term goals play their parts.

Short-term goals are like the stepping stones across a river. They're smaller, manageable chunks that you can achieve in days or weeks. They might involve simple actions, like exploring that park down the street you've always driven past but never visited. Or they could be a morning hike, practicing your camping setup, or taking a guided beginner's outdoor class. These bite-sized aspirations make the larger ones feel possible—they're proof you're capable, setting the stage for what's next.

Then there are long-term goals. These are your North Stars, the big ones. They may take months or even years to achieve. Picture yourself finishing the Camino de Santiago in Spain, joining an alpine climbing course, or even just mastering the art of preparing for a multi-day camping trip. Long-term goals often require more than just physical readiness—they involve planning, patience, and grit. But here's the great thing about them—every short-term goal you hit along the way builds momentum toward the final prize.

Think about Ravi, a dad who spent most of his 30s juggling family life and career demands. When his kids got a little older, they begged to go on an "adventure," so Ravi set a long-term goal for the family to complete a two-night backpacking trip together in the nearby Cascades. His short-term goals—including scout trips to the trail and assembling gear bit by bit—helped him prepare without feeling overwhelmed. When the day finally came, accomplishing that "big dream" wasn't just fulfilling—it changed how his family saw themselves. They weren't just city dwellers anymore—they were explorers.

## How to Set Goals That Speak to You

Goal-setting isn't just about making plans—it's about making plans that matter. A vague desire to "get outside more" isn't very powerful. But "hike three trails by the end of the season" is specific, actionable, and motivating. Great goals share a few key traits:

1. **They're Clear and Specific**
   Ambiguous goals can leave you floundering. Instead, break them into defined steps you can follow. For example, if you want to "get in shape for hiking," decide exactly how often you'll train, what type of trails suit your level, and when to schedule your outings.
2. **They Build Gradually**
   An achievable goal doesn't discount ambition, but it accounts

for where you are now. If summiting something massive like Mount Rainier feels too intimidating at first, start by tackling smaller peaks and scaling up over time.

3. **They're Aligned with Your Why**

   The best goals reflect what motivates you. If you're seeking mental clarity over physical challenges, you might prioritize quieter trails or meditative solo walks.

4. **They're Flexible**

   Life rarely sticks to plan. Maybe a storm delays your first camp-out, or an injury pauses your trek training. That's okay. Goals can adapt, and pivoting doesn't mean failure. It means resilience.

## Staying Inspired on the Journey

Even the most motivated adventurers face moments where the fire burns low. Maybe you get busy, the weather's ugly, or the doubts creep in. These moments are when it's most important to reconnect with your why.

Try keeping a journal of your adventures, where you jot down how those first steps felt and what you experienced. If your progress feels slow, revisit what you've already achieved to remind yourself of your growth. And don't underestimate the power of small celebrations—whether it's a coffee after a hike or a photo shared with friends, acknowledging your wins can keep you excited.

Sometimes, the key to motivation is external—not just celebrating your achievements solo, but finding like-minded adventurers to share them with. Joining a hiking group, asking a friend to meet you on the trail, or even shooting a quick message to someone who inspires you can reignite your momentum. Outdoor goals often thrive in community. After all, stories are best told to someone listening.

## What This Looks Like in Real Life

One small tweak can lead to a big adventure. Take Sofia, a stressed-out nurse, who was hesitant about hiking alone. Her first "goal" was just to walk her city park once a week. That tiny commitment eventually snowballed into trail-running events and weekends spent scaling forest ridges she never imagined herself attempting. Or Zack, who hated gyms but loved mountains. Over one determined year, he built a goal of hiking weekly after work, even in colder months, and has since conquered elevations he once feared.

Adventures aren't just about reaching a peak—they're about creating new habits and perspectives. Every day, you inch closer to something remarkable.

## The First Steps Toward Your Next Big Goal

You don't need to have all the answers right now. Clarity builds as momentum grows. Start by thinking about what excites you most—what new horizons are calling your name? Give yourself permission to dream big but know that every successful adventure begins exactly the same way—with a single step forward.

## Recap — A Few Key Takeaways:

1. Adventure goals succeed when grounded in personal motivations. Your "why" is what keeps you going.
2. Breaking big dreams into short-term and long-term goals makes them manageable and achievable.
3. Clarity, adaptability, and connection to your core reason for adventuring are the hallmarks of strong ambition.
4. Staying motivated is about tracking milestones, celebrating progress, connecting with others, and revisiting why you started.

## Try This:

- Write down your reason for wanting more adventure—it only needs to make sense to you.
- Define one small goal you can do this week; describe what it will involve and why it excites you.
- Dream a little bigger. What's one long-term adventure that lights your imagination?

Every summit begins with an idea, a step, and a willingness to try. What's yours going to be?

# Part II: The Foundations—Essential Outdoor Basics

# Chapter 4: Core Outdoor Skills & Safety

Every adventure—big or small—depends on one vital element: safety. It's what allows you to enjoy each moment with confidence, knowing you're ready to handle whatever comes your way. Core outdoor skills aren't just a box to check on your preparation list—they're tools that empower you to explore, adapt, and thrive in the great outdoors.

Whether you're planning a casual day hike or a multi-day expedition, these foundational skills will serve as your safety net. They are equal parts practical and adaptable, ensuring that you're prepared to enjoy nature responsibly while safeguarding yourself and those around you.

## The Navigation Basics

The wilderness can feel like an endless maze if you don't know how to find your way. Even well-marked trails can have forks, turns, or sections where signage is less clear. That's why navigation is one of the most critical outdoor skills to master—long before you lace up your boots.

The foundation of navigation is learning how to use a **map and compass**. While modern GPS devices and apps are convenient, they're not infallible. Batteries die, devices fail, and cell service drops. A map and compass, however, are always reliable.

Start small by familiarizing yourself with your map at home. Find the legend (it tells you what all those squiggly lines and symbols mean) and identify key features, like contour lines that show elevation. Practice orienting your map by lining up its north with the compass needle, and use landmarks like hills or bodies of water to match the map to the landscape around you.

Take Sarah, for example, a new trekker who learned this skill by marking a local trail on a map and practicing in her neighborhood park. Even though her "landscape" included streetlights and playgrounds, she gradually grew confident enough to apply her skills on an actual trail.

The goal isn't perfection; it's preparedness. A small amount of time spent learning to read a map and use a compass can be a true lifesaver.

## Fire-Building

Few things connect you to the outdoors like sitting around a fire, but fire also serves critical survival purposes—it provides warmth in cold conditions, makes food preparation possible, and, in emergencies, acts as a signal for help.

When it comes to fire-building, preparation is everything. The three basic elements of a good fire are **tinder, kindling, and fuel**. Start with tinder, like dry leaves, small twigs, or even a bit of tissue. Once the tinder catches, gradually add thin sticks of kindling to strengthen the burn, and then move on to larger logs as your base.

But building a fire isn't just about technique; it's also about responsibility. Always select a safe location, such as a designated fire pit or cleared area free of overhanging branches or dry vegetation. And never, under any circumstances, leave a fire unattended.

Sarah's first fire-building attempt taught her an important lesson—her choice of damp wood made starting the flames nearly impossible. By the time she eventually coaxed the fire to life, she'd learned firsthand why preparation matters, as well as how to keep a backup supply of dry tinder in a watertight bag for future trips.

## First Aid Essentials

Picture this scenario: You or a fellow adventurer trips over a protruding root, leaving a nasty scrape or twisted ankle. What happens next depends on your preparedness. First aid is about being ready not just for the predictable injuries, like blisters or scratches, but for the unexpected too.

Your first aid kit should be simple yet effective. Include bandages, gauze, antiseptic wipes, adhesive tape, pain relievers, tweezers, and any personal medications. It's also smart to brush up on basic first aid steps, like how to clean a wound or stabilize a sprain.

Emma, a casual hiker, once faced a scary situation when someone in her group suffered a mild allergic reaction during a trail lunch. Thanks to her kit (stocked with antihistamines) and quick thinking, the day's hike was able to continue.

Even as a beginner, you don't need to become an expert medic. However, taking a basic first aid course or wilderness first aid class equips you with the knowledge to respond calmly to injuries, giving you and others peace of mind.

## Understanding Weather

Weather can be one of the most unpredictable aspects of any adventure. Though sunshine can feel inviting, conditions can change dramatically—turning calm trails into risky terrain.

One of the most important skills you can develop is learning to read weather patterns and forecasts. This means planning ahead by checking reports, understanding cloud changes, and noting temperature drops. Carry appropriate clothing for any condition, remembering that weather in higher elevations tends to shift more quickly.

Take Greg, a first-time solo camper. A forecast of cloudy skies turned into a cold drizzle because he had failed to recognize rain signals, like darkening clouds and cooler afternoon breezes. Armed with that experience, his next trip included a waterproof jacket and an earlier camp setup time to avoid being caught out in the rain.

Preparation beats panic. Understanding how weather behaves helps you stay in control, even when nature is unpredictable.

## Risk Assessment and Emergency Planning

One of the most effective ways to stay safe is by **assessing risks before you start your adventure.** Even a seemingly simple activity, like a short hike, can present challenges. Consider these questions before setting out:

- What hazards might I encounter (e.g., steep terrain, strong currents, wildlife)?
- Does everyone in the group have the fitness and gear needed for the activity?

- What's the backup plan if the route is closed or we take longer than expected?

Emergencies happen, even to the best-prepared adventurers. That's why carrying essentials like a headlamp, emergency whistle, and firestarter can make all the difference. Practice situational awareness—always know where you are, stick to trails when possible, and maintain communication with your group.

Casey and her small hiking group once found themselves out later than expected after missing a trail fork. Thanks to their headlamps and shared map, they backtracked to locate the right path. From that moment, they learned the value of having contingency gear and staying calm in unfamiliar situations.

## Practicing Leave No Trace

Adventure isn't only about enjoying the environment; it's also about preserving it for future explorers. Following the **Leave No Trace** principles ensures that nature remains as pristine as when you arrived. This includes simple habits, like carrying out your trash, staying on trails to avoid damaging plants, and respecting wildlife from a distance.

Remember, the beauty of nature is fleeting when mistreated. By practicing Leave No Trace, you not only safeguard the environment but also inspire others to do the same.

## Recap — Core Skills

1. Navigation with a map and compass is a key skill every adventurer should master to stay safe and confident.
2. Fire-building is not only a survival tool but also a lesson in preparation and responsibility.
3. Basic first aid skills can make you a valuable resource on the trail and ensure small mishaps don't turn into big problems.

4. Reading weather patterns helps you adapt to changes and avoid potentially dangerous conditions.
5. Assessing risks, preparing for emergencies, and practicing Leave No Trace principles are essential for safe and responsible adventuring.

## Action Steps

1. Grab a local trail map and practice orienting it with a compass at home or in a nearby park.
2. Put together a basic first aid kit, or ensure your existing one is complete.
3. Review the Leave No Trace principles online and commit to one small habit change, such as switching to reusable containers for snacks.
4. Try building a small campfire (where it's safe and permitted) on your next trip to feel confident in the process.

Building core outdoor skills isn't just about safety; it's about growing your confidence and making every adventure more enjoyable. These tools are your foundation—your ticket to exploring with freedom and peace of mind. What skill will you try first?

# Chapter 5: Fundamental Gear & Packing

Packing for an adventure is an art form. Get it right, and you're prepared for whatever wonders and surprises nature has in store. Get it wrong, and your dream hike can quickly turn into an uncomfortable slog—or worse, an unsafe situation. But don't worry; packing doesn't have to be overwhelming. By understanding the fundamentals of gear and mastering a few strategies, you can approach it with the same ease as planning what to grab for lunch.

Whether you're heading out for a two-hour trail hike or a multi-day expedition, one concept anchors all your preparations: **The Ten Essentials**. These are the must-haves that ensure you're ready for the expected and the unexpected, giving you the freedom to focus on the adventure ahead.

## The Ten Essentials

The concept of the Ten Essentials emerged decades ago and remains just as relevant today. These items cover the core needs of outdoor activities—navigation, protection, warmth, light, safety, sustenance, and shelter. Here's what you need to know about each one:

1. **Navigation:** A map and compass are your foundation. While GPS devices and apps can be great, you should always have analog tools—and the knowledge to use them—because batteries die and devices fail. A basic compass and a waterproof map of your destination weigh almost nothing but can save you from wandering down the wrong trail.
2. **Sun Protection:** Sunglasses, sunscreen, and a wide-brimmed hat can protect your skin and eyes from harmful UV rays, even on cloudy days. Exposure can be sneakier—and stronger—at higher altitudes.
3. **Insulation:** Weather can change fast, especially in mountainous or remote regions. Always pack layers, including a waterproof jacket and an insulating mid-layer, like fleece or down. They don't take up much space in your pack but are vital if the temperature drops or rain rolls in.
4. **Illumination:** A headlamp or compact flashlight is a must, even if you're only planning to be out in daylight. Unexpected delays happen, and navigating in the dark without light can be dangerous. Don't forget extra batteries!
5. **First Aid:** A small but well-stocked first aid kit is your safety net for bumps, scrapes, and minor injuries. Customize your kit with essentials that match the specifics of your trip—like blister treatments for long hikes or antihistamines if you're sensitive to bug bites.
6. **Fire:** Matches or a reliable lighter (stored in a waterproof container) are essential for warmth, cooking, or signaling in an emergency. A backup like a firestarter or tinder (e.g., cotton balls dipped in petroleum jelly) is a smart addition.
7. **Repair Kit and Tools:** A multi-tool, duct tape wrapped around a water bottle, or a small sewing kit can patch up gear mishaps like torn straps or broken zippers. You don't need a full toolbox, but a few lightweight tools can save the day.
8. **Nutrition:** Pack more food than you think you need. Calorie-dense options like nuts, energy bars, and dehydrated

meals are easy to store and provide quick energy. On longer trips, consider foods that don't require cooking for emergencies.

9. **Hydration:** Start with a reusable water bottle or hydration bladder and research if the area has water sources to refill. A small water filter or purification tablets can make untreated water safe to drink. Don't underestimate how much water your body loses during physical activity, even in cool weather.
10. **Emergency Shelter:** You might never need it, but being prepared with a lightweight tarp, bivvy sack, or emergency blanket can mean the difference between a minor delay and a major ordeal if you're stranded overnight.

These essentials can be tailored to the specifics of your trip, but the core idea remains the same—they're your safety net.

## Packing Smart—The Balance of Weight and Function

It's tempting to cram everything you might want into your pack "just in case." However, the goal isn't to be overprepared but to be prepared *efficiently*. Carrying too much can slow you down and strain your body, particularly on longer treks.

Begin by selecting multipurpose items. For instance, a down jacket can serve as both insulation and a makeshift pillow; a buff can double as a scarf and a headband. Think about what you can reuse or repurpose for multiple scenarios to cut down on weight.

When packing, consider these simple strategies to balance weight and functionality:

- **Prioritize Basics First:** Lay out your Ten Essentials as the non-negotiable core of your pack. From there, add only what aligns with your adventure—do you really need an extra book for a half-day hike?

- **Distribute Weight Wisely:** Pack heavier items, like food and water, close to your spine and higher up in your backpack. This maintains balance and reduces fatigue. Reserve outside pockets for items you need quick access to, like snacks or navigation tools.
- **Test Run Your Backpack:** Before any trip, load your pack and wear it around the house or on a short walk. This gives you a chance to spot weight imbalances or identify unnecessary items before you hit the trail.

Jenny, a beginner adventurer, discovered the value of testing her pack firsthand. On her first overnight hike, she carried duplicate sweaters and an excessive food stash, making every mile feel like a marathon. After training herself to pack light, she found her following trips more enjoyable—and with fewer unnecessary "luxury" items stuck at the bottom of her bag.

## Gear Choices for Different Adventures

Not every trip requires the same gear. A casual walk through a local park doesn't need the same level of preparation as a multi-day backcountry trek. Your gear should match the demands of your activity, environment, and duration.

For beginners, it's smart to focus on versatile gear rather than niche items. Start with quality over quantity—a well-made backpack, sturdy shoes, and breathable layers will get you further than owning specialized equipment you rarely use. And if the price of gear feels steep, look into renting equipment or buying secondhand through reputable shops or online marketplaces.

As Ashley learned on her third camping trip, not every piece of gear has to be name-brand or top-of-the-line. A gently used backpack from a friend worked just as well as her first rental, and by consulting experienced hikers for advice, she avoided overpaying for gear she didn't really need.

## Tips for Beginners

Starting your gear collection can feel like a significant investment, but it doesn't have to happen all at once. Here's how to get started without breaking the bank or feeling overwhelmed:

- **Try Before You Buy:** If you're unsure about certain gear, consider renting or borrowing from friends for your first outings. This approach lets you experiment and figure out what works for you.
- **Test Your Gear:** Practice setting up your tent, cooking on your camp stove, or assembling your water filter at home or in your backyard. Knowing how your gear works in a controlled setting saves precious time and stress on the trail.
- **Keep It Simple:** Focus on building a solid foundation with your Ten Essentials and slowly expand to more specialized items as your goals evolve.

## Recap – Packing for Success

1. The Ten Essentials (navigation, sun protection, insulation, illumination, first aid, fire, repair tools, nutrition, hydration, and emergency shelter) form the core of every smart pack.
2. Keep your gear lightweight and multipurpose to avoid overpacking while maintaining safety and functionality.
3. Match your gear to the specific needs of your adventure, and prioritize durability and versatility over trends or brand names.
4. Always test your pack and equipment before heading out—it builds confidence and avoids surprises.

## Action Steps

1. Create your own Ten Essentials checklist for your next adventure. Start with the items you already own, and note what you need to borrow or purchase.
2. Test a new piece of gear in your backyard—practice setting it up, using it, or packing it to ensure you're comfortable with it.
3. Pack your bag as if you were leaving for a trip tomorrow, and take a short walk with it to evaluate the weight and fit.

Your gear doesn't just carry you through the outdoors—it helps you thrive in it. Building your setup and learning how to pack effectively is part of the adventure itself. Over time, you'll refine and personalize your toolkit, making every trip more comfortable and enjoyable. The trail is calling—how will you answer?

# Chapter 5.1: Gear Examples

When building your adventure toolkit, it's easy to feel overwhelmed by the sheer volume of outdoor gear available. To help make things simpler, we're breaking down each of the Ten Essentials mentioned in Chapter 5 with tried-and-true product recommendations. These examples will give you a clear starting point, with details on specific brands, prices, and where to purchase them.

## Navigation

### Garmin GPSMAP 67

- **Why It's Great**: Reliable in dense forests and canyons, with excellent satellite reception and long battery life. It includes preloaded topo maps and 16GB of storage.
- **Price**: $490
- **Where to Get It**: Available at Amazon and Backcountry.com.

### Garmin eTrex 32x

- **Why It's Great**: A budget-friendly option with a barometric altimeter and electronic compass, ideal for beginners. Compact and lightweight for day hikes.

- **Price**: $273
- **Where to Get It**: Amazon and REI.

### Budget Option – Suunto A-10 Compass

- **Why It's Great**: A simple and sturdy beginner-friendly compass that pairs well with any map.
- **Price**: $25
- **Where to Get It**: Outdoor stores like REI or online retailers.

## Sun Protection

### Anetik Ultraguide Hooded Sun Shirt

- **Why It's Great**: Featherweight, breathable, and comfortable for long outdoor days. Includes a hood for full protection.
- **Price**: $120
- **Where to Get It**: Anetik.com.

### REI Sahara Shade Hoodie

- **Why It's Great**: Affordable with excellent UPF 50+ protection. Includes a unique drawstring hood for extra face and neck coverage.
- **Price**: $50
- **Where to Get It**: REI.

### Budget Option – Banana Boat Sport Ultra Sunscreen SPF 50

- **Why It's Great**: Affordable and effective sunscreen that protects against UVA and UVB. A great addition to your toolkit.
- **Price**: $7.99 (8 oz.)

- **Where to Get It**: Most pharmacies or online retailers like Amazon.

## Insulation

### Patagonia Nano Puff Jacket

- **Why It's Great**: Ultralight, packable insulation with synthetic fill to keep you warm even when wet.
- **Price**: $229
- **Where to Get It**: Patagonia.com or REI.

### Uniqlo Ultra Light Down Jacket

- **Why It's Great**: A budget-friendly, lightweight jacket with exceptional packability. Ideal for layering.
- **Price**: $79.90
- **Where to Get It**: Uniqlo stores or their website.

## Illumination

### Black Diamond Spot 400-R Headlamp

- **Why It's Great**: Compact and rechargeable with 400 lumens. Includes multiple modes and weather resistance.
- **Price**: $49.95
- **Where to Get It**: REI or Black Diamond's website.

### Fenix E12 V2.0 Flashlight

- **Why It's Great**: Small, lightweight flashlight with 160 lumens that runs on AA batteries.
- **Price**: $29.95
- **Where to Get It**: Online retailers such as Amazon.

# First Aid

## Adventure Medical Kits Ultralight/Watertight .7

- **Why It's Great**: Includes the basics for treating most trail injuries and is packaged in a waterproof pouch.
- **Price**: $29.95
- **Where to Get It**: REI or Adventure Medical Kits.

## DIY First Aid Kit

- **Why It's Great**: Build your own kit with items like bandages, antiseptic wipes, pain relievers, and tweezers to suit your trip's specific needs.
- **Price**: Varies

# Fire

## UCO Stormproof Matches Kit

- **Why It's Great**: Waterproof matches that light even in windy or wet conditions, stored in a durable container.
- **Price**: $8.99
- **Where to Get It**: Outdoor retailers like REI or online.

## Light My Fire Firesteel 2.0

- **Why It's Great**: Produces sparks up to 5400°F and works in all weather conditions.
- **Price**: $19.99
- **Where to Get It**: Amazon or outdoor stores.

# Repair Kit and Tools

## Leatherman Wave+ Multitool

- **Why It's Great**: Includes 18 tools, from knives to pliers, in a compact design. Perfect for trail repairs.
- **Price**: $119.95
- **Where to Get It**: Leatherman.com or REI.

## Duct Tape & Gear Aid Tenacious Tape

- **Why It's Great**: Versatile and lightweight fixes for gear tears and holes.
- **Price**: $10
- **Where to Get It**: Outdoor gear retailers or hardware stores.

# Nutrition

## Clif Bars

- **Why They're Great**: Compact, calorie-dense, and available in multiple flavors. Excellent for quick energy.
- **Price**: $1.99 per bar
- **Where to Get It**: Grocery stores, REI, or online.

## Mountain House Freeze-Dried Meals

- **Why They're Great**: Lightweight and easy to prepare by just adding water. Perfect for overnight trips.
- **Price**: $10-$12 per meal
- **Where to Get It**: REI or Amazon.

# Hydration

### Katadyn BeFree Water Filter Bottle

- **Why It's Great**: Lightweight and effective for filtering water on the trail.
- **Price**: $44.95
- **Where to Get It**: REI or Katadyn.com.

### Budget Option – LifeStraw Personal Water Filter

- **Why It's Great**: Simple, affordable, and ultralight for emergency use.
- **Price**: $17.95
- **Where to Get It**: Amazon or outdoor retailers.

# Emergency Shelter

### SOL Emergency Bivvy

- **Why It's Great**: Lightweight and compact, offering insulation and protection from the elements in emergencies.
- **Price**: $19.95
- **Where to Get It**: REI or Amazon.

### Big Agnes Tiger Wall UL2 Tent

- **Why It's Great**: A lightweight, full-featured backpacking tent for those planning more extended trips.
- **Price**: $449.95
- **Where to Get It**: REI or Big Agnes's website.

# Recap – Gear Examples

1. **Navigation** – Garmin GPSMAP 67 ($490) for premium use, or the budget-friendly Suunto A-10 Compass ($25).
2. **Sun Protection** – Anetik Ultraguide Sun Shirt ($120) and REI Sahara Shade Hoodie ($50).
3. **Insulation** – Patagonia Nano Puff Jacket ($229) or Uniqlo Ultra Light Down ($79.90).
4. **Illumination** – Black Diamond Spot 400-R Headlamp ($49.95).
5. **First Aid** – Adventure Medical Kits Ultralight/Watertight .7 ($29.95).
6. **Fire** – UCO Stormproof Matches ($8.99) and Firesteel 2.0 ($19.99).
7. **Repair** – Leatherman Wave+ ($119.95) and duct tape ($10).
8. **Nutrition** – Clif Bars ($1.99/bar) and Mountain House Meals ($10-$12).
9. **Hydration** – Katadyn BeFree ($44.95) or LifeStraw ($17.95).
10. **Emergency Shelter** – Big Agnes Tent ($449.95) or SOL Bivvy ($19.95).

## Tips for Choosing Gear

1. **Match Gear to Your Needs** – Buy for the type of adventure you're planning, whether it's a day hike or a multi-day trek.
2. **Prioritize Durability** – Look for gear that will last, especially for essentials like navigation tools or shelters.
3. **Start Small** – Build your collection over time, starting with versatile and budget-friendly items.
4. **Rent Before You Buy** – For expensive items like tents, try renting first to find what works for you.

With the right gear in your kit, you're ready to take on the wild with confidence. Which piece will you add to your checklist first?

# Chapter 6: Planning Logistics & Permits

Every great adventure starts with thorough planning. Sure, spontaneity can add excitement, but covering the essential logistics beforehand is what keeps your trip smooth and stress-free. From transportation and accommodations to securing permits and crafting a flexible itinerary, this chapter will guide you through the practical steps of turning your outdoor dreams into a well-prepped reality.

## Step 1: Laying the Groundwork

The first step to any adventure is deciding on the **who, what, when, and where**. Will this be a solo trip, a couple's retreat, or a group outing? What activities are you planning (e.g., hiking, fishing, camping)? When do you want to go, and where will it take place? These basic questions shape everything that follows.

**Timing Your Trip**

- **Seasons Matter**: Know the seasonal conditions of your destination. For instance, spring may signal wildflower blooms in some mountains but lingering snowpack in others.

- **Avoid Peak Crowds**: If possible, plan for shoulder seasons (just before or after the busy season). Popular trails and campgrounds fill up fast during holidays or weekends.
- **Plan for Weather**: Use reliable weather apps (like AccuWeather or Windy) to track conditions, and keep an eye on extended forecasts.

**Destination-Specific Research**

- Browse blogs, guidebooks, or forums like AllTrails or Reddit's r/backpacking for firsthand advice about your chosen location.
- Download maps of the area ahead of time via apps like Gaia GPS or Google Maps (with offline mode).

# Step 2: Transportation

Your transportation plan will depend on your destination's distance, accessibility, and terrain.

**Getting There**

- **Road Trips**: If you're driving, ensure your vehicle is in good shape. Regular maintenance such as oil changes and tire checks can save you from headaches later.
- **Public Transport**: If you're flying or taking trains, plan ahead for potential delays. Research local transportation (buses, taxis, or shuttles) to your final destination.
- **Adventure Vehicles**: For remote or rugged terrain, consider renting a 4x4 or vanlife camper to increase your flexibility.

**On-Site Travel**

- Think about how you'll get around once there. Will you need a bike to explore? Will you carpool with a group to cut costs?

# Step 3: Accommodations

Your choice of accommodations sets the tone for your trip—comfortable, rugged, or somewhere in between?

## Camping Options

- **Developed Campgrounds**: These often have amenities like restrooms, water, and picnic tables. Book as early as possible through platforms like Recreation.gov if permits are required.
- **Backcountry Camping**: For more secluded experiences, understand the rules and secure permits if necessary. Check whether campfires are allowed in your area.

## Other Lodging Options

- Cabins, hostels, or nearby hotels can be a great backup when conditions change unexpectedly. Websites like Airbnb, Campspot, or The Dyrt offer various options close to outdoor destinations.
- Some public lands offer rustic forest service cabins—perfect if you want shelter without losing that "outdoorsy" feel.

# Step 4: Understanding Permits

Permits are often required to hike, fish, or camp in protected areas like national parks or wildlife reserves. Researching and securing these permits in advance is crucial.

## Types of Permits

1. **Camping Permits** – Necessary for specific campgrounds or backcountry zones.
2. **Wilderness Permits** – Required for hiking or overnight stays in certain areas.

3. **Activity-Specific Permits** – For fishing, boating, or climbing (e.g., fishing licenses).
4. **Event or Parking Permits** – Some parks require permits for parking or group gatherings.

**Navigating Permit Systems**

- Visit official government or park websites like Recreation.gov or National Park Service websites.
- Be aware of **lotteries** for high-demand spots—popular destinations like Yosemite's Half Dome or The Wave in Utah often use a lottery system for fairness.
- If needed, consider hiring guides for activities like fishing trips in restricted zones or hikes requiring technical expertise—many include permits in their fee.
- Set calendar reminders for significant dates, as permits often become available six months to a year in advance.

## Step 5: Crafting a Flexible Itinerary

Having a plan is important, but so is preparing for the unexpected. Adventure involves adapting to unforeseen roadblocks like weather delays, trail closures, or even low energy after a long day!

**Plan A and Plan B**

- **Outline Main Goals**: What are your trip's must-dos? For example, reaching a summit may be non-negotiable, but which trail you take can be flexible.
- **Alternative Destinations**: Research backup options in case your primary plan doesn't work out.

**Think About Time Buffers**

- Leave wiggle room for rest, meal breaks, or waiting out storms. Building buffer time into your schedule can prevent stress.

**Coordinating with Others**

- If traveling with a group, share your itinerary with everyone via shared documents (Google Docs works great). Agree on meeting points and timelines in advance.

**Tools and Apps for Planning**

- **Trail Apps**: AllTrails, Gaia GPS, or National Park interactive maps for route details and updates.
- **Weather Apps**: AccuWeather and Windy for real-time conditions.
- **Permit Platforms**: Recreation.gov for federal reservations, or Fish and Wildlife agency sites for localized permits.

# Recap – Planning Logistics & Permits

1. Start with solid groundwork—know your group, activity, timing, and location.
2. Plan your transportation, including contingencies for travel delays or on-site needs.
3. Choose accommodations that fit your trip, from established campgrounds to remote backcountry spots.
4. Research necessary permits early, monitor availability windows, and consider guided options when needed.
5. Create a flexible itinerary with realistic timeframes and alternatives for unforeseen changes.

## Action Steps

1. Select a destination and write down its permitting requirements, transportation details, and lodging options.
2. Use a tool like AllTrails or Gaia GPS to create your itinerary and download trail maps.

3. Mark permit dates on your calendar and aim to secure them as soon as they're available.
4. Double-check weather forecasts and adjust plans as needed.
5. Share your finalized plans with a trusted person or group to ensure everyone is aligned.

With your logistics and permits squared away, you're one step closer to a successful adventure. Now, it's time to lace up your boots and explore the vast possibilities ahead. Where will your next trip take you?

# Part III: Gear, Tech & Monetization

# Chapter 7: The Gear Revolution of 2025

Outdoor adventuring in 2025 is no longer just about hitting the trail with the basic essentials. Thanks to a wave of innovation, the gear we use has become smarter, lighter, more sustainable, and more versatile than ever before. These advancements aren't only for niche explorers; they're reshaping the experience for adventurers of all skill levels and preferences. From revolutionary cooking gear to AI-powered safety tools, this chapter dives into the cutting-edge trends and products fueling what we call "The Gear Revolution of 2025."

## Sustainable Gear for a Greener Future

Outdoor enthusiasts today want their footprints to be seen on trails, not on the environment. Sustainability has taken the spotlight, with more eco-conscious brands creating gear that minimizes environmental impact while boosting functionality.

### Examples of Game-Changing Sustainable Gear

- **Cotopaxi Allpa 35L Travel Pack**
    - Made with repurposed nylon that reduces waste while offering robust durability.

- **Practical Use**: Perfect for both urban adventures and rugged trails.
- **Price**: $200
* **Nemo Hornet Osmo Tent**
  - Constructed using entirely PFC-free water-repellent materials and made with recycled fabrics.
  - **Why It's Revolutionary**: Combines sustainability with high-performance weather resistance and ultralight portability.
  - **Price**: $449.95
* **Klean Kanteen Stainless Steel Bottle with New Sport Cap**
  - Produced with 90% recycled stainless steel and a new leakproof cap with a stainless steel straw.
  - **Usage**: Ideal for keeping you hydrated without harming the planet.
  - **Price**: $34.95

Sustainability doesn't compromise performance anymore. These products prove you can have ethically-made gear without sacrificing the quality adventurers rely on in the field.

## High-Tech Meets High Trails

The outdoor industry has embraced the tech revolution, making it easier than ever to safely venture into the unknown. Smart technologies like AI integrations, IoT-enabled devices, and real-time feedback systems are reshaping how explorers interact with their environments.

### Top Innovations in Smart Outdoor Gear

* **Garmin Epix Pro GPS Watch**
  - Features a built-in AI coach, pulse-ox monitoring for high altitudes, and detailed navigation with topo maps.

- **Best For**: Mountains, deserts, or any terrain where staying on track is critical.
- **Price**: $799.99
- **LifeFuels Smart Water Bottle**
  - Tracks your hydration levels via an app and lets you mix electrolytes or flavor pods at your convenience.
  - **Price**: $125
- **Petzl IKO Core Smart Headlamp**
  - Adjusts its brightness automatically based on ambient light and tracks remaining battery life through an app notification.
  - **Price**: $89.95

These devices not only help plan routes and monitor weather but also optimize performance and safety, allowing adventurers to manage their journeys with confidence.

# Ultralight Design—Big Performance, Small Weight

Lightweight gear has always been important for reducing fatigue, but advancements in material science have redefined what's possible. From shelters to cooking equipment, ultralight designs are helping adventurers push their limits without carrying unnecessary weight.

## Examples of Ultralight Trailblazers

- **Sea to Summit Ether Light XT Insulated Pad**
  - Weighs only 17 oz but provides unparalleled comfort and insulation.
  - **Price**: $199.95

- **Big Agnes Fly Creek Carbon Tent**
    - At just over 1 lb, it's one of the lightest tents on the market. Built with durable Dyneema fabric.
    - **Price**: $999.95
- **Campingmoon S1000 Ultralight Kettle**
    - Made with lightweight aluminum alloy, this kettle boils water quickly while keeping your pack light.
    - **Price**: $39.99

The ultralight revolution eliminates the traditional tradeoff between convenience and comfort, enabling adventurers to go farther, faster, and with less strain.

# Innovations in Must-Have Necessities

While high-tech gear grabs headlines, advancements in basic necessities continue to elevate the adventure game, proving that even the small details matter.

## Cooking Tools and Versatile Camping Gear

- **Campingmoon Portable Gas Stove with Flow Adjustment**
    - Compact and powerful, with adjustable heat for precision cooking.
    - **Price**: $75.99
- **Campingmoon Collapsible Fire Pit**
    - Portable yet sturdy, this stainless-steel fire pit ensures a safe and controlled fire for cooking or warmth. Packs down into a small, transportable size.
    - **Price**: $129.99
- **Leatherman Signal Multitool**
    - A 19-tool multitasker designed for outdoor adventures, featuring fire-starting tools, sharpeners, and built-in pliers.
    - **Price**: $129.95

These updates to classic tools demonstrate that essential gear doesn't need to be static—it can evolve alongside technological advances to improve utility and safety.

## Broad Trends Shaping 2025 Adventures

Beyond the specific products, overarching trends are defining the outdoor space for a wider variety of adventurers, from casual day hikers to extreme alpinists.

### Personalized Outdoor Experiences

Smart tech is making personalization a reality. Devices like the Garmin Epix Pro GPS Watch analyze your physique and habits to adapt recommendations for your specific needs.

### Urban Outdoor Trends

Gear and apparel now bring trail-ready durability to city life. Brands like Afends and RAB are blending streetwear aesthetics with high-performance fabrics, letting adventurers transition seamlessly from mountain trails to coffee shops.

### A Focus on Mental Wellness

Brands are recognizing the mental health benefits that outdoor recreation brings. Companies like Helinox are even introducing compact games and social accessories—like packable Yutnoris—that encourage bonding around the campfire.

## Recap – Carving the Path Forward

1. **Sustainability Leads the Way** – With gear made from recycled and biodegradable materials, the environmental impact of adventuring is shrinking.
2. **Advanced Tech Tools** – From AI-integrated watches to light-sensitive headlamps, technology is streamlining outdoor preparedness.
3. **Featherlight Gear** – Innovations in materials are allowing adventurers to go ultralight without sacrificing performance.
4. **Updated Essentials** – Everyday tools like stoves, multi-tools, and fire pits are smarter and more versatile than their predecessors.

## Pointers for Staying Ahead in the Gear Revolution

1. **Follow the Discussions** – Keep up with forums such as Reddit's r/Outdoors and trusted sites like OutdoorGearLab.
2. **Attend Trade Shows** – Events like Outdoor Retailer showcase the newest products before they hit the shelves.
3. **Sign Up for Updates** – Subscribe to newsletters from brands like Patagonia, Black Diamond, and Nemo for product launches.
4. **Seek Expert Reviews** – Check blogs and YouTube channels for hands-on gear tests and comparisons.

2025 is a vivid reminder of just how dynamic and versatile the outdoor gear landscape has become. By staying connected to these innovations, you're not just investing in products—you're investing in better, safer, and more memorable adventures. The next chapter of outdoor exploration is here—are you ready to step into it?

# Chapter 8: Filming & Content Creation

Capturing your outdoor adventures is more than just a way to create memories—it's an opportunity to share your story, inspire others, and even make a creative impact. With the latest advancements in technology, almost anyone can produce high-quality visual content. Whether you prefer to record with your smartphone or explore professional equipment, 2025 offers tools, techniques, and AI-driven solutions that elevate content creation to new heights.

## Tools for Capturing the Journey

### Smartphone-Based Filming

The everyday adventurer doesn't need heavy gear to create stunning visuals. Today's smartphone cameras rival professional equipment in quality and convenience.

- **iPhone 16 Pro Max**
    - Equipped with a 48MP camera, enhanced low-light capabilities, and ProRes 4K filming.
    - **Best Feature**: Its Cinematic mode offers depth-of-field effects for professional-looking videos.

- **Samsung Galaxy S25 Ultra**
  - Features a 200MP sensor and AI-driven stabilization for silky-smooth shots.
  - **Perks**: Advanced zoom capabilities to capture distant landscapes or wildlife up close.
- **Accessories**
  - Pair your smartphone with a **DJI OM 6 Gimbal Stabilizer** ($159) for smooth, shake-free footage.
  - Invest in a clip-on mic like the **Shure MV88+ Video Kit** ($249) for crystal-clear audio recording.

For most adventurers, the smartphone is the ultimate device—it's always in your pocket, intuitive to use, and packed with editing tools right out of the box.

## Advanced Filming Gear

For those seeking professional-grade results, 2025 brings cutting-edge cameras and drones designed to perform in the wild.

- **GoPro Hero13 Black**
  - Ideal for action-packed footage with 5.3K video and HyperSmooth stabilization.
  - **Best For**: Capturing extreme sports or underwater adventures.
  - **Price**: $399
- **Sony ZV-1 Mark II**
  - Designed for content creators, this compact camera excels in vlogging with 4K video and background blur for cinematic effects.
  - **Price**: $899
- **DJI Air 3S Drone**
  - Offers dual-camera mounting capabilities, 4K HDR, and extended battery life for capturing breathtaking aerial views.

- **Price**: $1,099
- **Peak Design Travel Tripod (Aluminum)**
  - Lightweight, compact, and sturdy, perfect for backpackers and minimalists.
  - **Price**: $379

## Editing Software Reimagined

Editing no longer takes hours of work; new tools and apps streamline the process, using automation to make professional-quality results accessible to everyone.

- **CapCut** (Free, Pro version $12/month)
  - Popular for TikTok and Instagram users, CapCut simplifies dynamic video editing with AI-powered features like auto-captions, background music matching, and cut detection.
- **Adobe Premiere Pro** (Starts at $20.99/month)
  - A veteran in the editing world, now incorporating **AI Scene Edit Detection**, suggesting the best cuts and transitions.
- **Runway ML** (Free and Paid Plans Available)
  - A new AI-driven editing platform that enables tasks like removing objects, color grading, or generating video effects with minimal effort.
- **LumaFusion** (iOS/Android, $29.99)
  - A robust mobile editing app for creators prioritizing portability.

# AI and The Future of Filmmaking

AI technology has transformed the way content is conceptualized, created, and shared. Here are a few ways to incorporate it into your adventure storytelling.

## Idea & Outline Generation

AI tools like **ChatGPT-4** or **Jasper AI** can help brainstorm scripts, storyboard ideas, or generate themes for your videos. For example, if you're planning a hiking vlog, ask the AI to suggest a filming sequence, from "packing preparations" to "reaching the summit."

## Automated Storytelling

Apps like **Pictory** or **Magisto** analyze your raw footage, automatically selecting highlights, syncing music, and adding text or transitions for seamless storytelling.

## Voiceover & Subtitles

AI-powered platforms such as **Descript** or **Deepdub** make it easy to add voiceovers or auto-generate subtitles for accessibility, complete with editing features that match tone and volume with your scenes.

## Personalized Editing

AI integration in smartphones and cameras helps elevate the editing process. For instance, the iPhone 15 Pro Max uses machine learning algorithms to suggest edits or fine-tune colors, making your videos look as polished as possible without needing professional expertise.

What was once labor-intensive now feels collaborative, with AI evolving into a powerful assistant for content creators.

# Ethical & Legal Considerations

While it's exciting to film your adventures, it's equally vital to consider the impact on the environment, wildlife, and people around you.

## Drone Regulations

- Always **check local laws** for drone usage. Many national parks or highly trafficked areas enforce strict no-fly zones.
- Register your drone if required, and operate within legal altitude limits (typically under 400 feet).
- **Pro tip**: Apps like **AirMap** or **DJI FlySafe** provide up-to-date flight guidelines.

## Respecting Nature

- Avoid filming in sensitive or restricted areas (e.g., wildlife nesting grounds or cultural heritage sites).
- Follow **Leave No Trace** principles—don't disrupt the natural environment for the sake of a perfect shot.

## Permissions and Privacy

- Obtain permits for commercial shoots in parks or public spaces. Contact local administration to ensure compliance.
- Respect the privacy of individuals in your footage. Ask for explicit permission before sharing clips featuring identifiable people.

# Distributing Content

You've shot and edited your masterpiece—now what? Sharing it effectively can help you reach the right audience and inspire others.

## Platform-Specific Advice

- **TikTok**
  - Focus on short, dynamic videos in a vertical orientation. Use trending hashtags and interactive features (e.g., polls or Q&A).
  - AI insights optimize post times for maximum engagement.
- **YouTube**
  - Create categorized playlists like "Weekend Hikes" or "Camping Meal Prep" to build content hubs. Use tools like **TubeBuddy** for SEO optimization.
- **Instagram**
  - Leverage Reels for short videos and Carousels for storytelling through photos. An interactive caption or compelling Story will further boost your reach.

## Tips for More Engagement

1. **Narrate the Context** – Pair breathtaking visuals with stories that resonate emotionally. Share not just the "where" but the "why."
2. **Show Behind-the-Scenes** – Offer bloopers, gear explanations, or real-time struggles to keep it relatable.
3. **Collaborate** – Work with other adventurers or influencers to cross-promote your content.
4. **Aim for Consistency** – Post regularly, and keep your visual aesthetic aligned with your unique identity (color schemes, fonts, and mood).

# Recap – Building Your Content Creation Toolkit

1. **Smartphone or Advanced Gear?** Start with what you have—your phone is more powerful than you might think, but drones and other cameras offer additional creative possibilities for specific needs.
2. **Maximize AI Support** – Use smart apps, automated editing, and script-writing AI tools to reduce effort and increase quality.
3. **Always Be Responsible** – Prioritize ethical filming practices, ensuring no harm comes to wildlife, nature, or anyone involved.
4. **Distribute Smartly** – Tailor your content for each platform and engage actively with your audience to grow your storytelling reach.

## Action Plan for Your First Outdoor Film

1. Pick your filming device and ensure it's fully charged—whether it's your iPhone or DJI Mini 4 Pro Drone.
2. Write a simple script or outline using AI tools to map out key scenes.
3. Plan for morning or late-afternoon shooting for optimal lighting.
4. Use editing software like CapCut or Premiere to create engaging content—experiment with AI features!
5. Share it on your chosen platform, using captions and hashtags that align with your audience.

With the power of technology and the magic of nature, every adventurer has the potential to tell a story that inspires the world. The tools are in your hands—what will you create today?

# Chapter 9: Monetizing Your Outdoor Passion

Living your outdoor dream doesn't mean leaving financial worries behind, but the beauty of 2025 is that you can turn your outdoor expertise into real income while staying true to your love for adventure. Whether you're teaching bushcraft to beginners, showcasing the best new gear, or capturing epic trail shots, there are countless ways to monetize your passion. The key? Keeping it rooted in the outdoors while building a lifestyle you genuinely enjoy.

This chapter focuses on income streams tailored to outdoor enthusiasts, strategies to grow your unique outdoor brand, and how to strike the right balance between adventure and earning.

## Outdoor-Focused Income Streams

### Sponsorships with Outdoor Brands

Outdoor brands—from hiking gear companies to eco-friendly apparel lines—are always looking for real adventurers to promote their products authentically.

- **How It Works**
    - Sponsors provide free gear, a commission, or direct payment in exchange for showcasing their products in your content. Think hiking backpacks, adventure jackets, or eco-conscious gadgets.
- **Getting Started**
    - Build trust by sharing real-life experiences with products you already use. For instance, sharing a video of a tent setup in harsh conditions can catch the eye of outdoor brands.
    - Use your outdoor knowledge to provide value—post gear reviews, tutorials, or packing guides.
- **Pro Tip**
    - Focus on brands aligned with your values, such as companies developing sustainable gear or supporting conservation efforts.

## Affiliate Marketing for Outdoor Gear

If you're already sharing recommendations with your friends or followers, affiliate marketing is a natural next step.

- **How It Works**
    - Sign up for affiliate programs from retailers like Patagonia, REI, or Backcountry. Share affiliate links for gear you use, and earn a commission when others purchase through those links.
- **Content Ideas**
    - Create "Top 10 Winter Hiking Must-Haves" blogs or YouTube videos showcasing gear essentials for a specific purpose.
    - Use Instagram or TikTok to create short, engaging gear breakdowns.

- **Pro Tip**
    - Your authenticity is your strongest selling point. Only promote gear you've tested in real-world conditions.

## Freelancing in Outdoor Photography or Writing

Outdoor adventures often bring incredible stories and visuals, creating opportunities to sell your skills.

- **Photographers**
    - Sell high-quality trail photos to magazines, websites, or directly to brands for commercial campaigns.
    - Offer prints or stock images through platforms like Adobe Stock or SmugMug.
- **Writers**
    - Write trail guides, gear reviews, or editorial pieces for adventure blogs or publications. Freelance platforms like Upwork or specialized sites like Matador Network can help you connect with clients.

## Coaching Adventure Skills Online

Offer educational resources for those looking to follow in your adventurous footsteps.

- **What You Can Teach**
    - Create video tutorials on essential topics, such as beginner hiking tips, wilderness survival skills, ultralight backpacking techniques, or outdoor meal prep.
    - Lead virtual classes, such as "Planning Your First Multi-Day Hike."

- **Platforms**
    - Use sites like Teachable for structured courses or Patreon for subscribers who support your ongoing tutorials and field updates.
- **Real-World Example**
    - Offer bespoke trip planning consultations for first-time hikers, helping them select gear, routes, and training plans.

## Building Your Outdoor Brand

The outdoor niche is thriving, but to stand out, you'll need to carve out a clear place in the community while showcasing your unique perspective.

### Choosing Your Focus

Your outdoor brand should align with your true passions and expertise.

- **Ask Yourself**
    - What aspect of the outdoors excites you?
    - Are you a hiking aficionado? A wildlife photographer? A gear enthusiast?
    - What problem or question can you solve for others?
- **Example Niches**
    - "Budget-Friendly Family Camping Trips"
    - "Photographing Wildlife Safely in Remote Locations"
    - "Minimalist Gear Reviews for Light-Packing Hikers"

### Crafting Your Unique Voice

People don't just follow information; they connect with personalities.

- **Be Authentic**
  - Share both your achievements and challenges. Outdoor enthusiasts appreciate relatability; showing how you conquered blisters or faced unpredictable weather makes your experience more meaningful.
- **Lean Into Storytelling**
  - Turn scenic hikes into narratives—"I found this hidden waterfall after hours of climbing… here's how you can too."

## Building Community

Engage by sharing your love for the outdoors with like-minded individuals.

- **Social Media Tips**
  - Instagram for lush photography. Pinterest for packing guides and tips. TikTok for quick, dynamic outdoor clips.
  - Respond to followers' questions to build an interactive community.
- **Collaborate Strategically**
  - Partner with like-minded adventurers, coaches, or photographers to reach new audiences while creating engaging content together.

# Balancing Passion and Profit

Successfully earning from the outdoors means walking a tightrope between loving your adventures and running a business.

## Avoiding Burnout

- **Schedule Downtime**
  - Set aside days for pure adventure—no filming, no deadlines, just nature.

- **Batch Work**
  - Film or photograph content during one trip and schedule it for weeks instead of constantly juggling adventures and editing.

## Staying True to the Outdoors

Your audience follows you for your authenticity as an outdoor enthusiast. Don't lose sight of that.

- **Keep the Fun Alive**
  - Chase physical challenges or soulful nature moments off-camera. These experiences fuel your passion, enhancing the authenticity of the content you do create.
- **Choose Wisely**
  - Don't accept sponsors or projects that undermine your personal or environmental values—your audience will see through it.

## Time Management

Effectively dividing your time prevents your outdoor passion from becoming solely about business.

- **Pro Tools**
  - Apps like Notion help plan your week, set content goals, and manage deadlines.
  - Automate tasks with tools like Zapier, or hire a freelance assistant for time-consuming chores.

# Recap – Steps to Monetize the Outdoors

1. **Explore 100% Outdoor Revenue Streams**
   - Test sponsorships, affiliate marketing, or one-on-one outdoor coaching. Tailor these opportunities to what aligns with your skillset.

2. **Build a Brand That Stands Out**
   - Focus on your niche, craft personal stories, and create meaningful content for your audience.
3. **Prioritize Passion**
   - Elevate your appreciation for nature—don't lose the joy of adventuring in the pursuit of profit.

## Action Plan to Start Monetizing

1. Identify your niche by combining outdoor passion with a clear audience need.
2. Sign up for an affiliate program or brainstorm brands to pitch your next adventure stories to.
3. Pick one piece of content to create today—be it a TikTok Reel, YouTube review, or online guide.
4. Plan one adventure to film for coaching, reviews, or sponsored content.
5. Use free tools (like Canva or Adobe Express) to give your brand solid visual foundations.

Earning a living while doing what you love outdoors may sound like a dream, but with clear steps, it becomes entirely achievable. Your wild stories, hard-earned skills, and honest connection to the wilderness are your unique currency—for helping others, building community, and maybe even supporting your next great adventure.

# Part IV: Physical & Mental Conditioning

# Chapter 10: Fitness for Adventure

Preparing your body for the outdoors is just as essential as planning your gear or mapping your route. Whether you're tackling a challenging climb, hiking your first trail, or embarking on a multi-day trek, your physical readiness can make all the difference between an enjoyable adventure and an exhausting struggle. The great news? Anyone can condition themselves to take on wilderness challenges with the right plan and consistency.

This chapter explores the key areas of outdoor fitness—endurance, strength, and flexibility—along with tailored workouts, routines, and tools to help you track your progress as you build the stamina and power needed for every kind of adventure.

## Training Foundations

Adventures can put your body to the test by demanding long hours of effort, carrying heavy packs, or navigating rugged terrain. Focusing on these three pillars of fitness will ensure you're ready to rise to the occasion.

## 1. Endurance

Endurance is critical for any outdoor activity involving sustained effort, from hiking to skiing.

- **How to Train**
    - Start with cardio activities like walking, running, swimming, or cycling three to five times a week.
    - Gradually increase the duration and intensity of your sessions. For example, begin with 30 minutes of brisk walking and work up to an hour or more with added inclines.
    - Incorporate hill sprints or stair climbing to simulate elevation gains on a trail.
- **Outdoor Equivalent**
    - Hiking shorter trails with a light pack is a great way to build endurance while already doing what you love.

## 2. Strength

Building strength enhances your ability to carry gear, climb tough terrain, and stabilize on uneven ground.

- **Key Areas**
    - **Legs** for hiking steep trails or ascending rocks.
    - **Core** for balance and stability.
    - **Upper Body** for climbing or carrying heavier loads.
- **Exercises to Include**
    - Squats, lunges, and step-ups for leg stability.
    - Push-ups and planks for functional upper-body strength.
    - Weighted carries or resistance bands for building real-world muscle strength.

### 3. Flexibility

Outdoor adventures demand flexibility to avoid injuries while navigating dynamic movements, such as reaching, twisting, and climbing.

- **How to Improve**
    - Incorporate daily dynamic stretches, like hamstring swings and torso rotations, before workouts.
    - Dedicate at least 10 minutes for static stretching or yoga after each training session to enhance range of motion.

# Practical Training Routines

You don't need an expensive gym membership or fancy equipment to prepare your body for the outdoors. These minimalist workouts will give you everything you need, whether you're in the living room or a campground.

## Minimal-Equipment Home Workout

- **Circuit Example** (Repeat 3 rounds):
    1. **Air Squats** – 12 reps
    2. **Push-ups** – 10 reps (modify with knees if needed)
    3. **Plank Hold** – 30 seconds
    4. **Glute Bridges** – 12 reps
    5. **High Knees** – 30 seconds

Simple bodyweight movements create a solid foundation for any level of adventurer. Perform this routine twice weekly for improved overall strength and balance.

## Interval Training for Stamina

For boosting endurance and torching calories in minimal time, try high-intensity interval training (HIIT).

- **Sample Routine**
    1. **Sprint** or power-walk for 30 seconds.
    2. Follow with 60 seconds of slow jogging or walking.
    3. Repeat for 10-15 rounds depending on your fitness level.

This 15-20 minute session can simulate the quick bursts of energy demands you'll need for steep climbs or navigating uneven trails.

## Core-Building Essentials

A strong core prevents fatigue, improves posture with heavy packs, and boosts balance.

- **Quick Core Workout**
    - Plank Variations: 3 sets of 30-second basic planks, transitioning to side planks.
    - Russian Twists (with or without weight): 20 reps.
    - Bird Dogs: 10 reps (each side).

Add this session twice a week to any routine for powerful results.

# Progress Tracking

Tracking progress isn't just about seeing results—it's also a great motivator and a tool to refine your approach. Whether you prefer tech-driven solutions or old-school methods, progress tracking can keep you focused and accountable.

## Fitness Apps

Apps bring structure to your training, providing plans, progress tracking, and challenges tailored to adventurers.

- **Recommended Tools**
    - **Strava** for tracking runs, hikes, and cycling with GPS data.

- **Fitbod** for creating custom strength-building routines.
- **Aaptiv** for guided audio workouts focused on endurance and mobility.

## Wearable Tech

Smartwatches and trackers provide deeper insights into your fitness levels, making it easier to set and hit goals.

- **Consider These Models**
  - **Garmin Instinct 2X Solar** for detailed trail tracking and heart rate monitoring.
  - **Apple Watch Series 10 or Ultra 2** for customizable fitness tracking paired with intuitive software.

## Manual Logs

Prefer to keep it simple? A dedicated notebook or spreadsheet works wonders for jotting down workout details, progress photos, or even energy levels after adventures.

# Recap – Building Your Fitness for Adventure

1. **Master the Basics**
   - Focus on endurance, strength, and flexibility to create a well-rounded fitness foundation.
2. **Simplify Your Training**
   - Use no-cost, practical workouts you can do anywhere—whether at home or on the go.
3. **Track Your Progress**
   - Use fitness apps, wearable tech, or even a simple pen-and-paper log to keep improving.

## Action Plan to Get Started

1. Assess your current fitness level and choose a training plan specific to your needs (beginner, intermediate, or advanced).
2. Schedule 3-5 training sessions per week to cover the major fitness pillars.
3. Try one or more tracking tools to monitor your workouts and progress over time.
4. Incorporate short training routines into your schedule that align with your adventure goals, whether that's hitting a mountain trail or tackling multi-day treks.

Outdoor fitness is about more than getting in shape—it's about empowering yourself to explore further, handle challenges more confidently, and fully enjoy all the breathtaking moments awaiting you in nature. With a plan, consistency, and the right tools, you'll not only prepare for adventure but thrive in it. The trail is calling—are you ready to take that first step?

# Chapter 11: Nutrition & Peak Performance

Fueling your body and taking care of your recovery aren't just side notes in outdoor adventures—they're the foundation that can turn a grueling trek into a joyful experience. Imagine being halfway up a mountain, your energy lagging, and realizing you packed nothing but candy bars. Or waking up with muscle aches because you skipped that post-hike stretch. It's moments like these that remind us how much the little decisions we make about food, hydration, and recovery shape our adventures.

This chapter is here to help you feel prepared, energized, and ready for whatever trail, climb, or expedition you take on next. From what to eat to how to recover, it's all about finding simple, sustainable habits that work for your outdoor lifestyle.

## Eat for Adventure

When you're outdoors, your body is working overtime. You're climbing, walking, balancing—every movement demands energy. That's why eating right is so important. But don't worry—you don't need to overhaul your entire diet. Instead, focus on practical tweaks that keep you fueled and ready.

## The Energy Trio

Think of your food as fuel. Every great adventure starts with three key macronutrients—carbohydrates, protein, and fats. Here's how they work together for your outdoor escapades:

- **Carbs are your battery**. They're your main source of energy. Before big adventures, opt for slow-burning carbs like oatmeal or whole grains. On the trail, quick fixes like dried fruit or granola bars can keep your energy steady when you start to slow down.
- **Protein is your repair kit**. Every time you climb, carry, or trek, your muscles do some heavy lifting. Protein helps them recover and get stronger. Chicken, tofu, eggs, and beans are solid choices for your base meals, while jerky or trail-friendly protein bars can fill the gaps in between.
- **Fats are endurance fuel**. These pack densely-caloric punch and are perfect for longer trips. Think nuts, seeds, nut butter packets, or even dark chocolate—it's not just delicious; it's efficient.

Ultimately, it's about balance. Pack meals and snacks that mix these nutrients so your body has what it needs to go the distance.

## Hydration Essentials

When you're outdoors, water isn't just a nice-to-have—it's survival fuel. Dehydration can zap your energy, fog your thinking, and make everything feel harder.

The rule of thumb? Aim for at least half a liter of water per hour of moderate activity. On hotter days or longer treks, add electrolytes to the mix. Electrolyte tablets, sports drinks, or even a pinch of salt with a squeeze of lemon in your water can keep fatigue and muscle cramps at bay. If you're heading far from fresh water sources, make sure you've got a lightweight filter or purification tablets.

And a quick tip for the forgetful among us—sip often. Waiting until you're thirsty means you're already playing catch-up.

## The Micronutrient Edge

Vitamins and minerals often get overlooked, but they can make a big difference between feeling strong and fighting fatigue. Vitamin C and iron boost energy and keep your immune system ready—look to foods like oranges, bell peppers, and leafy greens the night before a big outing. Don't forget magnesium, found in bananas and almonds, which helps keep those muscles from cramping up when you hit mile seven of your hike.

# Meal Prep That Works

Food on the trail doesn't have to mean soggy sandwiches or endless peanut butter wraps (though we do love a good PB&J when it's done right). With a little planning, you can eat well without overloading your pack.

## Real-World Snack Packing

Picture yourself halfway through a hike. You're sweaty, a bit tired, and you can feel the telltale gurgle of hunger kicking in. This is where smart snacking saves the day.

Trail mix is the classic, and for good reason—it's effortless. But variety is key. Consider adding freeze-dried fruits, chocolate pieces, or spiced chickpeas to keep every handful exciting. Pack nut butter packets for a quick energy boost with apple slices or crackers—they're basically adventure spreadables.

And if you're craving something savory? Bring along roasted seaweed snacks or cheese sticks. Bonus points for foods that don't require refrigeration.

### Easy Trail Meals

When it comes to meals, simplicity is your best friend. Dehydrated or freeze-dried meals are lightweight and reliable, but for an added DIY touch, pre-pack your own.

A personal favorite? Overnight oats mixed with protein powder and dried fruit—throw in hot water at camp and you've got a warm, filling breakfast. For dinner, pre-cooked rice packets paired with vacuum-sealed tuna and soy sauce can feel surprisingly gourmet when you're miles from civilization.

If you're camping and have the luxury of some fresh ingredients, wraps stuffed with sautéed veggies, cheese, and pre-cooked chicken can be pulled together on a portable stove. A sprinkle of spices (you can pack them in tiny containers) adds instant flavor without bulk.

### Save Weight, Add Value

Think about condensing flavor and calories. Small packs of olive oil, powdered hummus, or bouillon cubes are lightweight but high impact. They'll add depth to your meals without adding weight to your pack.

## Recover Right

The work isn't done once the hike or climb is over. How you recover shapes how your body performs on the next adventure—whether it's next week or tomorrow morning. Recovery isn't just for athletes; it's for anyone who loves waking up ready to move again.

### Rest and Repair

Good sleep is magical. It's the time when your muscles rebuild, your mind clears, and your energy resets. But when you're camping or sleeping in a new environment, it's easy to skimp on rest.

Invest in a high-quality sleeping pad that suits your terrain, and make sure your sleeping bag matches the nighttime temperatures you'll face. Bring an eye mask and earplugs if noise or light tends to wake you up.

If sleep still feels elusive, establish a simple bedtime routine—stretch out sore muscles, drink a calming tea, and hit the sack at the same time each night.

**Movement for Recovery**

Recovery is active, too. Post-adventure stretching can do wonders for tired legs and stiff shoulders. Focus on long, deep stretches for your calves, hip flexors, hamstrings, and lower back.

On longer trips, bring a small massage ball or roller. Spending just five minutes massaging your legs or upper back can help ease tension and keep you limber for the next day.

**Mindset Matters**

Finally, don't forget about mental recovery. Spending time outdoors is amazing, but it can also bring moments of stress—weather surprises, tough terrain, or just the sheer challenge of the day.

Practice mindfulness as you sit by your campfire or back at home. Write about your trip in a journal, from the highs to the lows, to help process your experience. Or simply take a moment to breathe deeply and reflect on the incredible spaces you explored.

# Take It All with You

At the end of the day, adventure is about balance—between pushing yourself and taking care of yourself.

- Fuel your body with balanced meals that work for you, mixing carbs, protein, and fats to keep you energized.
- Simplify meal planning with easy-to-pack snacks and adaptable trail meals.
- Always prioritize recovery, both physically and mentally, to hit the trails (or peaks, or rivers) feeling capable and enthusiastic.

Every bite, every stretch, every thoughtful moment of care is part of your preparation for the next adventure. The more you listen to your body and meet its needs, the more available you'll be to fully enjoy every step of the way. It's time to pack your snacks, roll out your map, and move with confidence into the wild. You've got this.

# Chapter 11.1: Examples and Recipes for Nutrition & Performance

When you're ready to fuel up for the outdoors, having a go-to list of reliable snacks, meals, and recovery tools takes the guesswork out of planning. Whether you're picking up pre-packaged options or whipping up something homemade, this chapter gives you practical ideas to keep your adventures powered.

We've also rounded up essential tools for cooking and recovery that are lightweight, effective, and budget-friendly. Here's your one-stop resource for building your ultimate trail menu.

## Snacks to Keep You Going

Snacks are the backbone of any adventure—they're quick, portable, and easy to eat on the go. These options will help you stay energized without weighing you down.

### Pre-Packaged Snack Options

1. **Clif Bar Energy Bars**
    - **Why it works**: High in carbs and moderate in protein, these bars are perfect for refueling during long hikes. Flavors like Chocolate Chip or Peanut Butter add variety.

- **Price**: $1.50–$2.00 per bar.
- **Where to get**: Amazon, REI, Walmart.

2. **RxBar Protein Bars**
    - **Why it works**: Made with simple ingredients, like egg whites and dates, providing clean fuel without added junk.
    - **Price**: $2.50–$3.00 per bar.
    - **Where to get**: Target, Whole Foods, online retailers.
3. **Trail Mix by Nature's Garden**
    - **Why it works**: Pre-made mixes with nuts, seeds, and dried fruits in resealable pouches. Ideal for one-handed snacking on the trail.
    - **Price**: $5–$8 per 16 oz bag.
    - **Where to get**: Costco, Amazon, specialty grocery stores.
4. **Justin's Nut Butter Packets**
    - **Why it works**: Individual packets of almond or peanut butter are handy for pairing with crackers or fruit.
    - **Price**: $1.00–$1.50 per packet.
    - **Where to get**: Walmart, REI, Thrive Market.
5. **KRAVE Beef Jerky (Black Cherry BBQ)**
    - **Why it works**: Packed with protein and comes in unique, flavorful options like black cherry. A lightweight, high-protein trail snack.
    - **Price**: $6–$7 per 3.25 oz bag.
    - **Where to get**: REI, Amazon, specialty retailers.

## DIY Snacks

- **Trail Mix Recipe**
    - **What you need**:
        - 1 cup roasted almonds
        - 1 cup dried cranberries
        - ½ cup dark chocolate chips
        - ½ cup pumpkin seeds

- Optional add-ons: coconut flakes, banana chips.
  - **Instructions**: Mix everything in a resealable bag or container. Adjust portions based on taste.
- **Homemade Energy Bites** (No-Bake)
  - **What you need** (makes ~12 bites):
    - 1 cup rolled oats
    - ½ cup almond butter
    - 2 tbsp honey (or maple syrup)
    - 2 tbsp chia seeds
    - ¼ cup mini chocolate chips
    - 1 tbsp cocoa powder (optional).
  - **Instructions**: Mix ingredients in a bowl, roll into bite-sized balls, and chill for 30 minutes before packing.

# Easy Camp Meals

On-the-go nutrition doesn't stop with snacks. A hearty meal can make all the difference after a long day of adventuring. Here are a mix of ready-to-eat and DIY meal solutions.

## Pre-Packaged Meal Options

1. **Mountain House Freeze-Dried Beef Stroganoff**
   - **Why it works**: Lightweight, high in calories (~500 per serving), and only requires hot water.
   - **Price**: $9–$10.
   - **Where to get**: REI, Amazon, local outdoor shops.
2. **Good To-Go Thai Curry**
   - **Why it works**: Offers bold flavors and clean ingredients without excess preservatives. Vegan-friendly.
   - **Price**: $10–$11 per pouch.
   - **Where to get**: REI, Backcountry, Good To-Go's site.

3. **Backpacker's Pantry Pad Thai**
   - **Why it works**: Slightly spicy, calorie-dense meal that balances carbs and protein.
   - **Price**: $12–$13 per pouch.
   - **Where to get**: Amazon, outdoor retailers.

## Simple DIY Camp Recipes

- **Quick Campsite Pasta**
  - **What you need** (for 2 servings):
    - 1 package of instant pasta.
    - 1 foil pack of tuna or chicken.
    - 2 tbsp olive oil or butter.
    - Dried herbs like basil or oregano (optional).
  - **Instructions**: Cook pasta according to package instructions using your camp stove. Mix in the tuna/chicken, olive oil, and herbs. Serve hot.
- **Breakfast Burritos**
  - **What you need** (for 2 servings):
    - 2 tortillas
    - 3 eggs, scrambled
    - Grated cheese (your choice, ~½ cup)
    - Pre-cooked veggies like peppers or mushrooms
    - Salsa packets (optional).
  - **Instructions**: Scramble eggs on your portable stove, layer them with cheese and veggies in the tortilla, and roll it up.
- **Overnight Oats for the Trail**
  - **What you need** (single serving):
    - ½ cup rolled oats
    - 1 scoop protein powder (vanilla pairs well)
    - 1 tbsp powdered peanut butter
    - 2 tbsp dried fruit (raisins or cranberries)
    - Hot water at camp.

- **Instructions**: At home, mix oats, protein powder, and peanut butter powder in a jar or bag. On the trail, add hot water, stir, and enjoy after 5 minutes.

## Recovery Tools and Essentials

Recovering from outdoor adventures doesn't require a lot of gear, but a few key products can make your downtime more effective. Here are some examples to consider.

1. **TheraBand Resistance Bands**
   - **Why it works**: Lightweight and portable, perfect for stretching and mobility exercises post-hike.
   - **Price**: $15–$20.
   - **Where to get**: Target, Amazon, sporting goods stores.
2. **TriggerPoint Grid Mini Foam Roller**
   - **Why it works**: Compact size makes it easy to carry, but still effective for massaging sore muscles.
   - **Price**: $25.
   - **Where to get**: REI, Amazon, direct from TriggerPoint.
3. **Garmin Instinct 2 Solar**
   - **Why it works**: Tracks physical activity, heart rate recovery, and helps monitor your performance outdoors.
   - **Price**: $399.
   - **Where to get**: Garmin's website, Best Buy, REI.
4. **GSI Outdoors Pinnacle Dualist Cook Set**
   - **Why it works**: Compact set includes pots, bowls, and mugs, designed for two and nests easily for portability.
   - **Price**: $70–$80.
   - **Where to get**: REI, Backcountry, Moosejaw.
5. **LifeStraw Peak Series Collapsible Squeeze Bottle**
   - **Why it works**: Combines hydration and purification in one compact tool—perfect for multi-day trips.
   - **Price**: $35.

- **Where to get**: Amazon, LifeStraw's website, outdoor retailers.
6. **Sea to Summit AlphaLight Camp Spoon**
    - **Why it works**: Lightweight yet durable, this spoon is perfect for dehydrated meals or camp cooking.
    - **Price**: $9–$10.
    - **Where to get**: Sea to Summit's website, REI.

## Wrap-Up

Planning for adventure nutrition and recovery doesn't have to be overwhelming. By mixing trusted pre-packaged options with easy DIY recipes, and investing in a few top-notch tools, you can eat well, stay hydrated, and recover effectively no matter where your path leads. Stock your pantry, pack your gear, and head outdoors knowing you're ready to fuel and restore like a pro.

# Part V: Adversity & Advanced Preparedness

# Chapter 12: Facing Worst-Case Scenarios

The beauty of the outdoors lies in its unpredictability, but that same unpredictability often brings challenges. Storms roll in without notice. Equipment fails at the worst possible moment. Wildlife decides to get a little too curious about your presence. Even in the best-planned adventures, things can go wrong. The good news? Being prepared means these moments are no longer disasters—they're simply obstacles you're ready to handle.

By learning how to anticipate dangers and respond calmly, you'll not only stay safe but also gain the confidence to explore further and deeper. This chapter lays out the tools, knowledge, and methods needed to face those "what if" moments with sure steps and clear strategies.

## Confronting Extreme Weather

Weather can change in an instant, and when it does, your survival often hinges on quick thinking and preparation. Here, we'll explore the on-the-ground realities of extreme weather and the steps you can take to safely handle each scenario.

## Storms and Lightning

Storms, especially those accompanied by lightning, can turn serene settings into high-risk zones. Imagine you're hiking on a ridgeline when the sky darkens, thunder rumbles, and lightning streaks across the horizon. What's your first move?

- **Get lower:** Head downhill or find lower ground. Avoid lone trees, ridges, and open spaces. Lightning tends to strike the tallest object in an area—don't be that object.
- **Crouch for safety:** If caught without shelter, assume the "lightning position"—crouch with your feet together, hands over your ears, and minimize ground contact to reduce the risk of ground current.
- **Avoid contact threats:** Keep metal gear, like trekking poles, far from your body. If you're wearing a pack with a metal frame, place it away and wait out the storm safely.

### Plan Ahead

- **Forecast first:** Check weather conditions for your route every morning. Apps like Windy or NOAA Weather Radar give real-time updates on storms and lightning risks.
- **Always pack a rain layer:** A compact, waterproof shell can keep you dry and warm, even in a surprise downpour.

## Flash Floods

Some of the most dangerous situations happen when floods strike without warning. Hikers near riverbanks or in canyons face the biggest risks as rising waters can wash out trails or engulf entire areas within minutes.

- **Signs of trouble:** Watch for sudden cloud buildups, unusual debris flow, or rapidly changing water levels. These often signal a flood in progress.

- **Immediate actions:** If water rises unexpectedly, move to higher ground fast. Never attempt to cross flooding rivers; even six inches of fast-moving water can knock an adult off their feet.

**Quick Tip:** Always study the topography of your route before heading out. Narrow canyons and valleys are prone to flash floods—have an exit strategy in mind.

## Wildfires

The smell of smoke or a faint orange glow is all it takes to raise alarm in wildfire season. Fires can travel at terrifying speeds, even across trails that seemed safe just minutes before.

**Steps to Stay Safe**

1. **Stay alert to fire updates:** Before heading out, check fire risk levels in your location using apps like Fire Weather & Avalanche Center.
2. **Plan your escape route:** Establish safe zones—large rock clearings, bodies of water, or dirt paths. If you spot smoke, move downhill into areas with little vegetation.
3. **Beware of smoke inhalation:** Protect your lungs by carrying a buff or mask you can moisten to reduce the impact of breathing in smoke.

## Other Natural Disasters

Sometimes, the ground itself becomes your greatest challenge. Hurricanes, earthquakes, and volcanic eruptions are some of the rarest scenarios but demand specific preparations.

## Hurricanes

If weather forecasts indicate high winds or incoming storms, minimize risk by canceling trips to exposed terrains or coastal regions. Always adhere to evacuation orders and have waterproof gear to protect essentials.

## Earthquakes

Stay clear of cliffs, loose rocks, or areas susceptible to landslides. Drop to the ground during shaking, shielding your head and neck while keeping away from snapping branches or falling debris.

## Volcanic Eruptions

Always orient yourself away from valleys where lava flow typically follows. Protect yourself from dense ash clouds with a basic dust mask or a damp cloth over your nose and mouth.

# Managing Wildlife Encounters

Sharing the wilderness means respecting the creatures that call it home. Most animals want as little to do with you as you do with them, but knowing *how* to react can make all the difference for those rare close encounters.

## Bears

The sight of a bear lumbering across your path can feel surreal—until it starts moving toward you. The first rule of bear country is prevention. Secure your food in scent-proof bags and store it in bear canisters far from your sleeping area. When hiking, travel in groups and make noise to avoid startling bears.

- **Black Bear:** If you encounter one, stand tall, wave your arms, and speak firmly. If it continues to approach, use bear spray when it's within 25 feet.
- **Grizzly Bear:** Avoid eye contact and back away slowly. If a grizzly charges, drop to the ground in a fetal position, protecting your neck, and play dead.

## Mountain Lions

Rare but intimidating, mountain lions stalk prey and can be aggressive if startled. To handle a confrontation, make yourself appear larger—raise your arms, yell loudly, and maintain eye contact. Do not run or crouch, as this can trigger their chase instincts.

## Snakes

Venomous or not, most snakes strike only when they feel threatened. Watch where you step, especially near rocks or in tall grass. If bitten, stay calm and keep the affected limb immobilized while seeking emergency medical help immediately.

**Pro Tip:** Leave snakes alone! Most bites occur when people attempt to move or provoke them.

# When Gear and Tech Fail

Even the best-planned trips can be derailed by failing equipment. How do you keep going when your boots buckle or your GPS battery dies miles from the trailhead?

- **Navigation:** Carry a physical map and compass, and practice basic orienteering before your trip. Apps are great until your phone runs out of battery.

- **Fix-it kit:** Include duct tape, zip ties, and multi-purpose tools like a Leatherman. Duct tape can seal tears in fabric, repair boots, or even hold broken tent poles.

**Realistic Backups**

- *Battery run-outs?* Invest in a lightweight power bank ($25+) or a solar charging kit for multi-day treks.
- *Water filter fails?* Always pack water purification tablets as a secondary option.

**Tip:** Test your gear at home to avoid mishaps on the trail.

# Emergency Protocols

Preparation isn't just about carrying the right gear—it's about knowing how to act when every second counts.

## First Aid Must-Haves

A properly stocked first aid kit can mean the difference between minor discomfort and a serious problem. Some essentials include bandages, antiseptic wipes, pain relievers, antihistamines for allergic reactions, tweezers, and an emergency thermal blanket.

## Rescue Beacons

If your adventure takes you off the grid, a personal locator beacon like the Garmin inReach Mini can be a lifesaver. These gadgets allow you to signal rescue services even when there's no cell service. Make sure you're familiar with how to activate it and practice sending a test message.

**Evacuating Safely**

Above all, remember to stay calm. Panic burns precious energy and clouds judgment. If forced to evacuate, leave markers like flagging tape or written notes showing your direction of travel. Move slow and methodical toward rescue points like roads or streams.

## Closing Thoughts

Venturing outdoors is about finding freedom, but freedom requires preparation. Extreme weather, curious wildlife, or unexpected tech failures don't have to overshadow your adventures. With knowledge, tools, and a steady mindset, you'll not only survive the unexpected—you'll come back with stories of triumph. Always pack your essentials, study your route, and be ready to problem-solve on the fly. Your adventures have just begun.

# Chapter 13: Responsible Adventuring & Community

Adventure has a way of connecting us—not just to nature, but to each other. There's something uniquely unifying about reaching the same summit, spotting the same sunrise, or overcoming challenges together. But adventuring isn't solely about personal growth or ticking boxes off a bucket list. It's also about the impact we leave behind, the relationships we build, and the role we play in preserving the wild spaces we love.

Being a responsible adventurer starts with mindfulness. Whether it's respecting local ecosystems, investing in the communities we visit, or guiding others toward their own outdoor journeys, every choice we make adds up. This chapter explores how to tread lightly on the earth, find your community, and give back, turning your love of the outdoors into something larger than yourself.

## Environmental Stewardship

Every trip we take—no matter how small—leaves a trace. The question is, how much of that trace is positive, and how much creates harm? Responsible adventuring isn't just about enjoying what nature offers; it's about preserving it for future generations.

# The Principles of Leave No Trace

The Leave No Trace (LNT) philosophy isn't just a set of rules—it's a mindset. The seven principles guide adventurers to minimize our impact, whether you're out for a day hike or a multi-week expedition:

1. **Plan Ahead and Prepare:** Know the area you're visiting. Research regulations, expected weather, and fragile ecosystems. For example, not all campsites allow open fires due to the risk of wildfires or damage to vegetation.
2. **Travel and Camp on Durable Surfaces:** Stick to established trails and campsites to avoid trampling delicate areas. A patch of grass might look resilient, but a single misplaced tent can damage decades of regrowth.
3. **Dispose of Waste Properly:** Carry out everything you carry in—including food scraps, which can disrupt wildlife habits. For human waste, dig a cat hole at least 6 inches deep and 200 feet away from water sources.
4. **Leave What You Find:** Resist the urge to pocket that beautiful rock or colorful plant. Instead, snap a photo and leave it untouched for the next visitor.
5. **Minimize Campfire Impact:** Fires are beautiful but often unnecessary. Stick to stoves for cooking, and if fires are permitted, use pre-existing fire rings instead of building new ones.
6. **Respect Wildlife:** Feeding or approaching animals disturbs their natural behavior and can be dangerous for you and them. Observe from a distance using binoculars or a zoom lens.
7. **Be Considerate of Others:** Share the trails responsibly by yielding to uphill hikers, keeping noise levels down, and packing headphones for music.

## Respecting Local Cultures

When exploring internationally—or even just visiting a far-off region of your own country—you're stepping into someone else's home. Respect for local customs, traditions, and people is at the heart of responsible adventuring.

Take the time to learn about the area's history and culture. For instance, in some regions, access to certain peaks or trails may be sacred to Indigenous communities. Always seek permission before venturing into restricted areas. A little research can prevent unintentional disrespect and even lead to richer cultural experiences.

**Pro Tip:** While in remote or rural areas, make an effort to support local businesses—buy your gear or snacks at small shops, eat at locally-owned places, and stay in family-run accommodations whenever possible. It keeps the community economically resilient while reducing the environmental impact of large-scale tourism.

## Eco-Friendly Practices

Every adventurer can reduce their footprint by making smarter choices about what they bring and how they travel.

- **Gear Sustainability:** Opt for quality gear that lasts longer, reducing waste from lower-quality items. Companies like Patagonia and REI offer repair services for damaged gear.
- **Low-Waste Packing:** Use refillable containers, ditch single-use plastics, and plan meals to minimize leftover waste. For instance, premix spices or trail snacks at home in reusable bags instead of buying individually wrapped items.
- **Transportation:** When possible, carpool to trailheads or use public transportation to reduce emissions—an especially great way to meet others with the same adventuring mindset.

By being intentional with our choices, we can reduce harm while still fully enjoying the outdoors.

## Finding Your Tribe

Adventuring alone has its charm, but being part of a community can elevate it. Whether you're seeking wisdom, companionship, or just someone to share a sunset with, there's no shortage of ways to connect with like-minded explorers.

### Online Platforms for Adventurers

Technology has made it easier than ever to connect with others who share your passions.

- **Forums and Social Media Groups:** Websites like Backpacking Light or Reddit's r/Outdoors are treasure troves of advice, trip reports, and even meet-up opportunities. Local Facebook or Meetup groups often organize group hikes for beginners and veterans alike.
- **Apps for Adventure Buddies:** Platforms like AllTrails or HikingProject allow you to not only plan your trips but connect with others who've hiked the same routes or those looking for companions.

### Local Clubs and Organizations

Joining a hiking, climbing, or paddling club in your area is one of the most accessible ways to find like-minded adventurers. These groups frequently host events, trips, and skill-building workshops. Plus, they're an excellent avenue for learning about trails or activities you hadn't considered before.

For example, volunteering for local trailwork organizations like a branch of the Sierra Club or Appalachian Trail Conservancy can connect you to others while actively giving back to the environment.

## Group Tours and Volunteering

For larger adventures—such as high-altitude treks or extended international expeditions—group tours provide structure, shared expense, and camaraderie. Companies like G Adventures or Wildland Trekking specialize in group experiences that balance adventure with responsible travel practices.

Volunteering opportunities, whether maintaining trails or planting trees for conservation, offer purpose alongside exploration. Programs like REI's stewardship events or non-profits like Leave No Trace combine community building with tangible action.

**Personal Note:** Some of the strongest trail friendships blossom while shoveling dirt to rebuild eroded sections of track or untangling invasive species from beloved parks. Nothing strengthens bonds like shared sweat equity.

# Paying It Forward

Once you've carved your path through the wilderness, why not turn around and lend a hand to the next adventurer? Responsible adventuring isn't just about what we take from nature but what we give back.

## Sharing What You've Learned

There's a steep learning curve for newcomers to the outdoors, but your experiences—what worked, what didn't, the lessons learned along the way—create a foundation for others. Share trail recommendations, gear tips, or preparations you wished you'd known about on your first trip.

Host workshops at local libraries or through clubs to teach navigation, safety, or Leave No Trace ethics. Writing detailed trail reviews or recording video guides on platforms like YouTube can inspire and educate far beyond your local circle.

## Mentoring the Next Generation

Imagine being someone's first introduction to the outdoors. Mentoring a friend, family member, or even a new hiking buddy can spark a lifelong love of nature.

- Take a curious co-worker on a short day hike.
- Help someone train for their first overnight trek.
- Share resources like beginner-friendly gear rentals or step-by-step guides.

## Joining Conservation Efforts

From trail restoration to wildlife management, there's always work to be done, and outdoor lovers are perfectly positioned to help. Organizations like The Nature Conservancy, Leave No Trace Center for Outdoor Ethics, or even local land trusts rely heavily on volunteers.

Donating to or joining conservation projects isn't just a way to build skills—it's a tangible way to ensure future generations inherit the same wilderness we did.

# Closing Thoughts

When you adopt responsible adventuring practices and connect with a community, your trips take on a deeper, more enriching purpose. You become more than just a visitor in nature—you become a caretaker, a guide, and a voice for its preservation.

Every time you make the conscious choice to Leave No Trace, every time you teach someone to pitch their first tent, and every time you rebuild a washed-out trail, you're becoming part of something bigger. A shared love for adventure has the power to build bridges, restore landscapes, and inspire others to step outside their comfort zones.

The wild spaces are waiting, but they need us now more than ever. Take the lessons you learn in the outdoors and share them. Build a community. Protect the trails you tread. Because adventure isn't just about the places we go—it's about the footprints we leave behind.

# Part VI: Bringing It All Together

# Chapter 14: Crafting Your 2025 Action Plan

You've gathered your gear, honed your skills, and expanded your knowledge. Now, it's time to take everything you've learned and create a plan for your most epic outdoor adventures yet. Crafting an action plan isn't just about listing destinations or penciling in dates—it's about setting yourself up for success, staying motivated, and building in the flexibility to adapt when life throws you curveballs.

This chapter will help you design an action plan that covers every detail from choosing the right gear to sticking to your budget. You'll also discover ways to keep the excitement alive with motivational hacks and strategies to turn your 2025 adventure dreams into reality.

## Roadmap to Success

Achieving your adventure goals begins with breaking them into actionable steps. Think of your plan as a blueprint—it's the structure that will guide you from preparation to execution.

### Step 1: Define Your Adventure Goals

Start by envisioning what you want to achieve. Are you dreaming of completing a multi-day thru-hike, summiting a challenging peak, or spending more weekends exploring local trails? Write down your adventure goals in specific terms.

- **Example 1:** Instead of saying, "I want to hike more," set a goal like, "I will complete three new national park hikes by June 2025."
- **Example 2:** Replace "I want to camp" with "I will plan and complete a solo overnight at Yellowstone in late summer."

## Step 2: Build Your Gear Checklist

With your goals in mind, take inventory of your current gear. Determine what you already have, what needs upgrading, and what's missing. Focus on essentials first—sturdy boots, a reliable pack, weather-appropriate clothing, navigation tools, and a basic first aid kit.

### Creating a Budget-Friendly Gear Plan

- **Research:** Compare brands, reviews, and features to match your needs with your budget. Patagonia's Worn Wear or REI Garage Sales are great places to find quality used gear.
- **Rent Before You Buy:** For high-cost items like tents or climbing gear, rent them locally or through online services (like Outdoorsy or Gear Up) to test before making a purchase.

### Pro Tip

Build your list into categories:

- *Must-have high-priority* (e.g., trekking poles, water filter)
- *Upgrade later* (e.g., lightweight sleeping pad)
- *Optional* (e.g., high-end cooking accessories).

## Step 3: Create a Training Schedule

Every adventure requires preparation—both physical and mental. Tailor your training to the demands of your chosen activities. For trails, work on hiking endurance and terrain gradients. For kayaking, build upper body strength and practice water safety skills.

**Example Training Plan for a Summer Hike**

**January–February:** Begin with weekly day hikes, adding 2–3 miles each outing. Increase intensity with hill climbs or weighted packs.
  **March–April:** Join a weekend backpacking trip to practice carrying gear overnight. Focus on improving pace while handling elevation.
  **May–June:** Test key routes similar in terrain to your summer hike and refine your gear setup.

## Step 4: Budgeting Strategies

Your adventures don't have to break the bank. Make budgeting part of your action plan so you can explore without financial stress.

**Budgeting Checklist**

1. Estimate the total cost for gear, transportation, permits, and supplies for each trip. (Use trail apps to predict costs—e.g., the John Muir Trail permit fees or park entrance pricing.)
2. Separate savings goals by month. Use apps like Mint to organize.
3. Find ways to cut costs—pair up with friends for shared gas, opt for free campsites using resources like Recreation.gov, or utilize loyalty programs at outdoor retailers for discounts.

## Step 5: Set Timeline Goals

Timelines keep your goals on track. Take each adventure and reverse-engineer its timeline. For example:

- *Ultimate Goal:* Thru-hike the Appalachian Trail (June–August 2025)
- *Timeline*:
    - By January 2025, finalize permits and travel logistics.

- By March, complete gear setup and training benchmarks.
- By May, plan and test your resupply strategy.

Creating smaller milestones like this reduces overwhelm and ensures you're consistently progressing.

## Creating Flexibility

Even the best-laid plans can go awry—seasonal closures, sudden storms, or unexpected personal circumstances. Building a flexible approach into your action plan ensures you're ready to pivot without losing momentum.

### Backup Plans for Every Goal

1. **Gear Alternatives:** If a piece of gear breaks or isn't working well, know where to borrow or rent replacements temporarily.
2. **Seasonal Plans:** Prepare alternative adventures for different times of the year. If snow or heat makes one destination unsafe, have a cooler or warmer backup location ready.
3. **Shorter Swaps:** If conditions don't permit a multi-day trek, break it into smaller out-and-back routes or explore day trails instead.

### Adapting to the Unexpected

**Example Problem:** Two weeks before your planned trek, authorities close your destination due to wildfire risk.

- **Adapted Solution:** Shift to a coastline hike where conditions are unaffected. Use the prepared gear and resupply plans, tweaking only a few logistical details.

Flexibility allows you to stay on course for your adventure mindset, even when the specifics change.

# Motivation Hacks

Sticking to your action plan requires more than logistics—it takes consistent motivation to keep moving forward. Here are some hacks to stay excited and accountable throughout the process.

## Find Accountability Partners

Adventure buddies can help keep you motivated for training hikes, provide encouragement, and share the planning load. They can also prevent you from postponing goals simply because "life got in the way." Join a local group or use social media to find others working toward similar objectives.

## Join Social Media Challenges

Platforms like Instagram or Strava host seasonal outdoor challenge hashtags (#ChallengeYourTrail, #30DaysOutside) or events. Participating not only connects you with others but also helps you track milestones publicly—building momentum as you mark progress.

## Start an Adventure Journal

Documenting your preparation can do wonders for accountability and reflection. Use a notebook or a journaling app to log training steps, gear reviews, and even mental reflections about your upcoming trips.

**Pro Tip:** Set weekly or monthly goals in your journal. For instance:

- "This week, research rental options for snowshoes."
- "Complete 10 miles of hiking with a fully-loaded pack."

Reading back over your progress can be a motivating reminder of just how far you've come when the going gets tough.

**Celebrate Small Wins**

Every achievement in your action plan is worth acknowledging. Treat yourself to new hiking socks after completing a training milestone or celebrate finishing a challenging day hike with your favorite post-trail meal. Don't wait until the summit to recognize successes.

# Closing Thoughts

Your 2025 action plan is more than just a checklist. It's a roadmap, a motivator, and a promise to yourself. It turns dreams into steps, obstacles into opportunities, and goals into realities.

By planning intentionally, preparing for the unexpected, and finding ways to stay excited along the way, you're setting yourself up for success—and incredible memories. Whether your biggest adventure next year is your first solo overnight or the culmination of years of practice on a thru-hike, this plan will be your foundation.

Adventure is as much about the preparation as the moment itself, so enjoy every brainstorming session, every training mile, and every packed bag along the way. The wild spaces are ready for you. And now, you're ready for them.

# Chapter 15: Conclusion - Your VistaReady Future

Adventure is more than just an act. It's a mindset, a lifestyle, and a commitment to both the world around you and the person you want to become. You've come a long way since the idea of becoming VistaReady first crossed your mind. With this book, you've taken steps to transform curiosity into capability, dreams into plans, and plans into actions.

This isn't just a guidebook—it's the beginning of a new chapter in your story as an adventurer. Think of everything you've accomplished so far. You've developed the foundational skills to enjoy the outdoors safely and comfortably. You've equipped yourself with knowledge to handle unpredictable situations, and you've built the mentality to approach every challenge as an opportunity for growth.

But most importantly, you've pledged yourself to a purpose-driven way of adventuring. You're not just a guest in nature—you're an advocate, a steward, and now, part of a thriving community dedicated to preserving and celebrating the wild spaces we all cherish.

Today is the perfect time to pause, reflect, and celebrate your progress, but it's also a call to action—to keep learning, keep exploring, and keep becoming.

# Recap of Your VistaReady Adventure

Every chapter in this book has been carefully designed to help you step into the outdoors as your most prepared and resourceful self.

## A Mindset for Exploration

At its core, discovering the outdoors begins in the mind. You've learned that curiosity, resilience, and adaptability are some of the strongest tools an adventurer can carry. The first trail you conquer is the one in your head—the trail that tells you "I can." Now, equipped with courage and positivity, you're ready to scout the real trails that await you.

## Building Your Foundation

From understanding gear to choosing the right skills to master, you've laid a solid groundwork. You've learned how to research, pack, navigate, and step into the wilderness with confidence. Whether it's planning a simple day-trail adventure or a multi-day trek, you now know how to prepare for success and savor every moment of the experience.

## Facing Challenges with Confidence

The outdoors can be unpredictable, but it's what makes it thrilling. Through preparation, quick thinking, and the plans you've made to handle worst-case scenarios, you're ready to conquer any challenge. From navigating fierce weather to handling wildlife encounters, you've proven to yourself that you're capable of exploring with both safety and excitement.

## Adventuring with Purpose

Your pursuit of adventure isn't just about personal triumph—it's a gift to the world. Through Leave No Trace principles, respecting cultures, and giving back to conservation projects, you've embraced what it means to be part of something larger. Every responsible choice you make ensures the trails you love will be there for your children and their children, long after your footprints are gone. You've chosen to steward the future of adventure itself.

## Turning Dreams into Plans

The roadmap for 2025 is now in your hands. You've set goals, outlined actions, and filled your future with purpose and flexibility. With a well-thought-out plan and the drive to bring it to life, you've proven that any horizon can be reached with intention and effort. The wild places are no longer places you long for—they're destinations you know how to reach.

These lessons are more than just skills—they're a lifestyle to guide you in every new experience, every challenge, and every breathtaking view ahead.

# Looking Ahead

The end of one adventure is always the doorway to the next. Picture your future now. Do you see yourself standing on that first new summit? Paddling along mirrored waters at sunrise? Laughing around a campfire with new friends you met on the trail? The possibilities aren't just endless—they're yours for the taking.

Adventure isn't about being fearless—it's about stepping into the unknown with open eyes and a brave heart. It's about finding joy in both the peaks and the valleys, knowing that every challenge teaches something valuable.

Take what you've learned from this book and carry it with you. You're ready for the next step. The question is, what's calling you? Is it a high-altitude peak you haven't dared to try? A bustling rainforest alive with sounds and surprises? Or perhaps it's staying closer to home, exploring your local landscapes with fresh eyes. Whatever it is, approach it boldly. The world is waiting for your next chapter.

Remember, every trip into the wilderness offers something new—not just about the land but about yourself. The person who starts the trail isn't always the same as the one who finishes. And that transformation? That's what makes adventure legendary.

Your story is far from over. If anything, it's just beginning.

## Final Invitation to the VistaReady Community

You aren't just an adventurer—you're part of a movement. Across the globe, thousands of people just like you are discovering, exploring, and sharing their journeys in the wild. This thriving VistaReady community is one of shared wisdom, encouragement, and passion for the outdoors.

We invite you to continue that connection. Join the conversation, share your stories, and learn from others on the same path. Together, we are stronger, smarter, and more inspired than we could ever be alone.

Visit [www.vistaready.com](www.vistaready.com) to stay connected, access new resources, and keep your VistaReadiness alive. Whether you're looking for gear tips, planning your next big trip, or hoping to connect with fellow adventurers, the site is your hub for all things exploration.

We encourage you to share your triumphs, photos, lessons, and even mishaps—because every story you tell inspires someone else to step out and try. Post your adventure moments, join a conservation project, or invite a friend on their first trek. By sharing, we remind each other of why we love the wilderness and why it must be protected.

Your VistaReadiness isn't just about you—it's about the community you're building, the inspiration you're spreading, and the wild spaces you're protecting. Together, we're shaping the future of adventure.

## Take the Next Step

Your gear is ready. Your action plans are in place. And your community is here to walk—or climb, or paddle—alongside you. This conclusion isn't the end; it's an open invitation to explore more, care more, and share more.

The mountains are calling. The forests are alive with whispers of adventure. And the trails stretch ahead, waiting for your heartbeat, your vision, and your spirit.

Stay curious. Stay bold. Stay ready.

# Disclaimer

This publication is intended to provide general information and inspiration for outdoor enthusiasts. While every effort has been made to ensure accuracy and reliability, the content should not be taken as professional, medical, or legal advice. Always consider your personal fitness level, consult qualified experts when necessary, and follow local regulations and safety guidelines during any outdoor activity.

Portions of this book were developed with the assistance of artificial intelligence tools, in conjunction with the author's insights. The author has taken reasonable steps to review and refine the content for clarity and accuracy, but any errors or omissions remain the sole responsibility of the author. The experiences, strategies, and suggestions are based on personal perspectives and may not apply universally.

By reading this book, you agree that the author and publisher are not liable for damages or injuries arising from the use of the information provided.

No part of this publication may be reproduced, distributed, or transmitted in any form or by any means, including photocopying, recording, or other electronic or mechanical methods, without the prior written permission of the publisher, except in the case of brief quotations embodied in critical reviews and certain other noncommercial uses permitted by copyright law. For permission requests, write to the publisher:

VISTAREADY LLC

Email: info@vistaready.com

Website: www.vistaready.com

Become VistaReady: How to Prepare for the Season of Adventures. 2025 Edition.

Copyright © 2025 by John McHook

All rights reserved.

www.ingramcontent.com/pod-product-compliance
Lightning Source LLC
Chambersburg PA
CBHW081146060526
44107CB00135B/705